Spanish-Language Books for Public Libraries

Fabio Restrepo, editor
Erwin Buttler
Sylvia Flores Johnson
Isabel Schon
Martha Tome

ad hoc subcommittee of the
Library Services to the Spanish-speaking Committee
Reference and Adult Services Division
American Library Association

American Library Association
CHICAGO AND LONDON
1986

Cover design by Charles Bozett

Text design by Marcia Rasmussen

Text composed in Brother Spanish
  on an IBM PC Jr. Index composed
  on a Tandy 6000.

Printed on 50-pound Glatfelter,
  a pH-neutral stock, and
  bound in 10-point Carolina
  cover stock by
  Malloy Lithographing, Inc.

Library of Congress Cataloging in Publication Data
Main entry under title:

Spanish language books for public libraries.

    1. Bibliography--Best Books--Spanish imprints.
2. Public Libraries--Book lists. 3. Spanish imprints.
4. Acquisition of Spanish publications. I. Restrepo,
Fabio. II. American Library Association. Library
Service to the Spanish Speaking Committee.
Z1035.7.S7 1986   025.5'27763'08968   85-28940
ISBN 0-8389-0448-3

Contents

Introduction

The compilation of this bibliography was possible thanks to the combined effort of a five-member ad hoc subcommittee of the Library Services to the Spanish-Speaking Committee of the Reference and Adult Services Division of the American Library Association and a grant from the Carnegie Fund administered by the ALA Publishing Committee.

The idea for a similar project had been discussed in the past by many groups, committees, and individuals concerned about library service to the estimated 20 million Hispanics living in the United States and aware of the lack of bibliographic tools to aid in the selection of appropriate materials. Unfortunately, only a very limited number of attempts to provide librarians with those tools have been, if only partially, successful. For example, Proyecto LEER, initially a special branch of Books for the People Fund, Inc. and recently incorporated as a unit of the Texas Woman's University School of Library Science, has helped librarians and teachers to select educational and recreational materials through the **Boletín**; inadequate funding, however, has consistently made this publication extremely irregular and not appropriate as a selection tool for current materials in public libraries. The Arizona chapter of REFORMA published in 1978 **A Core Collection of Print Material for Libraries Serving the Spanish-Speaking of the Southwest,** a short and useful list of representative titles in several subject areas but, as the title indicates, of limited interest in other sections of the country. The list of Books in Spanish which occasionally appears in **Booklist** serves mostly as a report of items received by the Donnell Foreign Language Library of the New York Public Library. About two years ago the El Paso Public Library started issuing **La Lista**, añ acquisitions list with short annotations and price information, but it doesn't satisfy the needs of libraries wanting to build a basic collection. Another recent entry in the field is **Lector**, a review publication of the California Spanish Language Data Base which includes materials suitable for all types of libraries but is of limited usefulness to the average librarian searching for a solid basis upon which to develop an authoritative collection of Spanish materials.

At the 1981 ALA Annual Conference in San Francisco, the RASD Committee on Library Services to the Spanish-Speaking discussed the several alternatives available to librarians who need to develop a basic list of Spanish materials to better serve their Hispanic constituency. As a result, it decided to focus its efforts on the compilation of a bibliography of important literary and popular works, in addition to a carefully selected sample of materials available on a variety of topics that could be used around the country.

In view of the magnitude of the task and the possibility of acquiring grant funds for this type of project, the Committee submitted a proposal to the Carnegie Reading List Fund with the approval of the RASD Board. Prior to the 1982 Annual Conference in Philadelphia, the Committee received notification of the grant award.

Soon after the Conference, the process of selecting members for an ad hoc subcommittee to work on the list started. Criteria for selection included depth of knowledge of Spanish materials, experience in libraries or institutions dedicated to serving the bibliographic needs of the Spanish-speaking, and willingness to generously contribute time and effort to the project. An additional important factor was representation of the major Spanish groups living in the United States: Mexican, Puerto Rican, and Cuban.

The Subcommittee members selected were the following: Isabel Schon, Arizona State University, whose extensive background in children's and young adult Spanish literature includes several publications; Sylvia Flores Johnson, Spanish specialist, Los Angeles Public Library, and consultant in the field of library services to the Spanish-speaking, whose thorough knowledge of Spanish materials and the needs of the Hispanic user added immensely to the project; Martha Tomé, founder and director for several years of Proyecto LEER, who actively developed library services in Latin America as library specialist for the Organization of American States; Erwin Buttler, Spanish specialist, the New York Public Library, who has regularly contributed a list of

Spanish materials to **Booklist**; and Fabio Restrepo, assistant manager, Dallas West Branch, Dallas Public Library, former director of Proyecto LEER at Texas Woman's University School of Library Science, where he has taught courses on the selection and acquisition of Spanish-language library materials.

At the 1983 ALA Midwinter Conference in San Antonio, the subcommittee met for the first time to establish parameters for the project according to the terms of the grant, to determine what subject areas were truly basic and had to be included, and to assign responsibilities to members. Then, in May of 1983, the subcommittee met in Chicago to evaluate individual contributions. Each member made recommendations for inclusion, and the result was a preliminary list whose final version received tentative approval at the 1983 ALA Annual Conference in Los Angeles. At this point, a validating test was conducted to determine whether the list did include materials useful to libraries around the country. Copies of the list were sent to the Houston and Miami-Dade public libraries, and the librarians in charge of the Spanish collections there were asked to go over the list and recommend changes. The results of the test served to confirm the subcommittee's belief in the general applicability of the list.

The grant called for a list of approximately 500 items, with short annotations in English, directed primarily to adult audiences. The subcommittee felt that among the criteria established to include materials two were of outmost importance: literary merit and wide general appeal. In identifying subjects of wide appeal, this work may be said to make an original contribution. The interest in listing subjects of popular interest is more consistent than is the interest in identifying Spanish translations of the classics. Some works of literature and some on philosophy and other theoretical subjects were included only because they combined literary merit and popular appeal. Many others were omitted because popular interest was absent. The greater part of this basic list is devoted to providing suitable titles in popular subject areas. It must be noted, however, that in subjects of popular interest, one title may be as good as any other.

As it turns out, the list exceeds the 500-item limit established, but, as the process of compilation developed, it became obvious that the number of materials worth including, even for a basic list, far exceeded the original estimate. Users will surely find gaps in different areas. The subcommittee members are well aware of this fact and wanted to include many more items. It was determined, however, that

selected entries will serve well the needs of the average
library and thus achieve the purpose of this project.
The annotations are short and in English for two rea-
sons: first, the list includes only items recommended for
purchase, and all a librarian needs to make a decision is an
indication of the subject matter, coverage, context, or setting, rather than a lengthy critical review. Second, the
list seeks to facilitate the non-Spanish-speaking librarian's selection of materials, and therefore the use of English seemed most appropriate. In some cases, only the words
"translation of" and the original title appear in the anno-
tation. A user should then go to regular reviewing sources
for additional information about the item in question.

As already pointed out, the subcommittee felt that literary merit and wide general appeal were the two criteria
that would most accurately guide the selection of items for
inclusion. Traditionally, many collections of Spanish materials in U.S. libraries have been assembled without due
regard for the authority of the writer, the relevancy of
content, the quality of translation, or the true satisfaction of an expressed need. In most cases, the collections
consist of Spanish books purchased from the local bookstore
when a modest amount of library money became available, or
books that were donated anonymously to the library. Except
perhaps for the collections of major public libraries that
serve Hispanic communities, almost all collections are in-
significant compared to what is truly needed by the popu-
lation in the service area of the library.

Literary merit, of course, applies primarily to creative
writing. Therefore, the subcommittee set out to identify
the great Spanish writers of all times and countries and to
select from their production not only important but also
popular works in all genres--books that the average
individual should be familiar with and that most people will
enjoy reading. All five members participated and offered
suggestions for the chapter Literature and Rhetoric; while
the list is by no means complete, it does represent some of
the best of creative writing in Spanish.

The words "wide general appeal," as used in this bibliography, mean items that Hispanics--as witnessed by the subcommittee members who work in large public libraries--often
request and read. This criterion also suggests items that
the subcommittee members believe should be available at any
library that has significant numbers of actual or potential
Hispanic users. Some areas of knowledge, such as philosophy
and poetry, that are highly regarded and commonly liked by
the average Hispanic individual are not included in the collections of the typical library because many librarians are

not fully aware of the reading interests of their community.
Certain categories of materials--particularly in the areas
of religion, social sciences, language, art, and sports--
were included partially because of the widespread lack of
knowledge about their existence (as reported by several
members) but primarily because they are items without which
no public library serving Hispanics can properly function.

In a few instances, only one item has been included
under a subject. This was not intentional but it resulted
from the lack of materials of similar quality. In some cases, that item included is a textbook, and the inclusion had
as much to do with availability as with popularity. Students not proficient in English often have no alternative
but to read in their native language and textbooks used in
the United States have frequently been translated into
Spanish.

The majority of the materials in this list were suggested by Sylvia Flores Johnson and Erwin Buttler. Their suggestions certainly reflect the wide variety of interests expressed by the clienteles of two of the largest library systems in the nation. The Los Angeles Public Library serves
mostly a Mexican-American clientele and the New York Public
Library mostly Puerto Ricans, but both attract large numbers
of Hispanics from every Spanish-speaking country.

Isabel Schon suggested all the materials for young people regardless of the subject categories, and Martha Tomé,
Latin American fiction. Fabio Restrepo, besides his overall
responsibility for putting the project together, verifying
bibliographic entries, getting price information, and edit-
ing the entire list, made suggestions for inclusion or
deletion in almost all areas.

No doubt many users of this list will feel that some important items were left out and that a few irrelevant items
were included. The subcommittee members realize this and
admit the difficulty of satisfying all users. Perhaps future editions of the list should be more comprehensive, and
suggestions from many more sources included. Ideally, this
list should mark the beginning of a publication similar to
Public Library Catalog.

A special thank you is due several libraries that made
suggestions for the list: Houston Public Library (Carnegie
Branch), Miami Dade Public Library (Foreign Languages),
Atlanta Public Library (Humanities Division), Rochester,
N.Y., Public Library (Literature and Recreation Division),
Salt Lake City Public Library (Fiction and Literature
Department), Tucson Public Library (Spanish Services), Free
Library of Elizabeth, N.J., Bethlehem Public Library (South
Side Branch), Memphis-Shelby County Public Library, and

Phoenix Public Library (Language and Literature). The staff of the Los Angeles Public Library deserves special mention for the support given to this project.

The subcommittee would also like to thank Danuta A. Nitecki and Nathan A. Josel, Jr., for their contributions in drafting the successful grant proposal that made this list possible; Andrew M. Hansen, RASD Executive Director, for his continued support and encouragement and Patricia Squires for her patience, dedication and help during the typing and word processing stages of the project.

Arrangement
and Use

The list, arranged by Dewey Decimal Classification (19th edition), gives full bibliographic information, and price when available. A letter indicates price range and replaces a dollar amount because of the wide variation in bookdealer prices and the need to guide librarians in their expenditures. Letters stand for the following: A=over $20, B=between $15 and $20, C=between $10 and $15, D=between $5 and $10, and E=between $1 and $5. An asterisk (*) indicates an item every library should have. The letters HB designate a hardbound book.

Materials on this list were in print in 1984, and it is reasonable to assume that they are still available. However, because of the volatility of the Spanish book market, it is almost impossible to establish at any given time the availability of every item included. On the other hand, given the wide variation in stock size among distributors, it is recommended that buyers do not assume a title is out of print simply because one dealer is unable to supply it when ordered. Pricing practices also vary enormously from one distributor to another, and buyers should exercise caution in making purchasing decisions.

A few items in the 800 section do not include ordering (bibliographic) information. The subcommittee addressed this issue early in the project and decided there was no need for this type of data. In poetry, for example, the majority of authors listed are represented in anthologies. Librarians can therefore use the titles given to verify their inclusion in the anthology. Dealers should also be

able to provide individual titles, if desired. The section
Additional Authors does not include bibliographic citations
because the authors are easily recognized by most librarians, the books translated are the same that made the
bestseller list in English, and the distributors of Spanish
materials should not have any difficulty supplying them.

Biography and young adult fiction appear separately.
Spanish-language periodicals, some of them translations of
popular American titles, are listed in a supplement. A
second supplement lists dealers of Spanish-language materials as well as their specialties.

000 Generalities

032—ENCYCLOPEDIC WORKS

Enciclopedia Barsa de consulta fácil. México: Encyclopedia
  Britannica, 1981. 16v. HB. $A.
  Contains information useful in the United States.

Gran enciclopedia Rialp. Madrid: Rialp, 1981. 24v. HB.
  $A.
  One of the best encyclopedias in Spanish. Articles are
long, well-illustrated, and include bibliographies.

Larousse, Pierre. **Pequeño Larousse en color: diccionario
  enciclopédico de todos los conocimientos.** Paris:
  Larousse. 1978. 1564p. HB. $A.
  An excellent, well-illustrated one-volume encyclopedia.

McWhirter, Norris. **Guinness, libro de los records.**
  Barcelona: Catalana, 1983. 300p. $C.
  Translation of the **Guinness Book of World Records.**
Compilation of data on world records in a wide variety of
activities.

100 Philosophy and Related Disciplines

100—PHILOSOPHY

*García Tuduri de Coya, Mercedes. **Introducción a la filoso-fía.** New York: Minerva, 1973. 395p. $E.
Examines the history and nature of philosophical thought. Includes a chapter on the importance of philosophy in Latin America.

Marías Aguilera, Julián. **Introducción a la filosofía.** Madrid: Alianza, 1979. 352p. $B.
A classic and frequently requested history of philosophy, written by an important contemporary Spanish philosopher. Also published by Revista de Occidente.

*Ortega y Gasset, José. **¿Qué es filosofía?** Madrid: Alianza, 1979. 240p. $E.
This classic by one of the greatest Spanish thinkers, is both literary and philosophical. It enlightens but tends to digress.

103—DICTIONARIES, ENCYCLOPEDIAS, CONCORDANCES OF PHILOSOPHY

Enciclopedia de filosofía y filósofos. Madrid: Cátedra, 1979. 422p. (Colección Teorema: Serie Mayor). $C.

2

Translation of **The Concise Encyclopedia of Western Philosophy and Philosophers.** Includes terms, "isms," philosophers, and fields of philosophical inquiry.

109—HISTORY OF PHILOSOPHY

Durant, William James. **Historia de la filosofía.** México: Diana, 1978. 599p. $C.
Recreates the lives and times of the great philosophers.

*Marías Aguilera, Julián. **Historia de la filosofía.** Madrid: Revista de Occidente, 1979. 520p. $B.
A classic and very readable history of philosophy.

133—PARAPSYCHOLOGY AND OCCULTISM

Balanovski, Eduardo. **Los fenómenos paranormales; nacimiento de una nueva ciencia aplicada a los más antiguos mitos del hombre.** Barcelona: Gedia, 1982. 219p. $D.
An objective description of scientific tests conducted to verify paranormal occurrences.

*Holzer, Hans. **Manual de parapsicología.** México: Olimpo, 1978. 176p. $E.
A handbook on parapsychology covering extra-sensory perception, out-of-the-body experiences, life after death, reincarnation, witchcraft, Satanism, and other mysteries. Translation of **The Handbook of Parapsychology.** Also published by Picazo.

El libro supremo de todas las magias: los tesoros ocultos al alcance de todos. México: Saturno, 1970. 487p.
(Biblioteca ciencias ocultas) $C.
Arranged by white, red, black, and green magic, this very popular title in the Mexican community discusses astrology, folk medicine, divination, physiognomy, alchemy, magnetism, amulets, exorcism, and dream symbols. It also includes excerpts from the writings of Albert the Great, Hermes, and Cleopatra.

Scheffler, Lilian. **Magia y brujería en México.** México: Panorama, 1984. 175p. HB. $C.

This well-illustrated title describes the origins, rituals, and beliefs of witchcraft in Mexico.

133.1—Apparitions (Ghosts)

Maynard, Christopher. **Fantasmas.** Madrid: PLESA, 1979.
32p. (El mundo de lo desconocido). $E.
Appropriate for all ages, this well-illustrated, interesting work covers famous ghosts and ghost trackers.

133.3—Divinatory Arts

*Benavides, Rodolfo. **Dramáticas profecías de la Gran Pirámide.** México: Mexicanos Unidos, 1974. 413p. $D.
This book by a popular Mexican author studies prophecies based on the Great Pyramid of Cheops.

Bucheli Hagal, Elías. **El poder oculto de los números.** Buenos Aires: Kier, 1978. 223p. $D.
A serious study of numerology.

Douglas, Alfred. **El tarot.** Barcelona: Bruguera, 1976. 185p. (Libro amigo). $E.
Traces the origin and symbolism of the tarot cards.

*Gallotti, Alicia. **Nostradamus, las profecías del futuro.** Barcelona: Martínez Roca, 1981. 233p. (Fontana fantástica). $E.
Gallotti, a well-known journalist, interprets the Prophecies of Nostradamus, including references to the end of the world, the assassinations of John Kennedy, the Pope and Marilyn Monroe, and the coming of Napoleon and Hitler. Some of the interpretations are far-fetched, but the book is popular.

*Profecías de Nostradamus y San Malaquías.** México: Orion, 1978. 191p. $E.
Contains the text of the prophecies of Nostradamus and of Malachi.

*Toth, Max. **Las profecías de la Pirámide.** Barcelona: Martínez Roca, 1981. 266p. (Fontana fantástica). $E.
Prophecies based on the Great Pyramid of Cheops.

133.323—Radiesthesia

Graves, Tom. **Radiestesia práctica.** Barcelona: Martínez
Roca, 1981. 187p. (Fontana práctica). $E.
A translation of **Dowsing: Techniques and Applications.**
A practical manual for those who want to learn dowsing tech-
niques.

Moine, Michel. **Radiestesia.** Barcelona: Martínez Roca,
1980. 319p. $D.
The history and uses of dowsing.

133.32424—Cartomancy by Tarot

Douglas, Alfred. **El tarot.** Barcelona: Bruguera, 1976.
185p. (Libro amigo). $E.
Traces the origin and symbolism of the tarot cards.

133.5—Astrology

Astrología: ¿vieja superstición o nueva verdad? Madrid: Altalena, 1980. 90p. $D.
A popular overview of astrology written in collaboration
with G. L. Driscot, the famous astrologer.

*Goodman, Linda. **Los signos del zodíaco y su carácter.**
Barcelona: Pomaire, 1977. 619p. $B.
Translation of **Sun Signs.** Describes each astrological
sign and discusses its compatability with others.

Parker, Derek. **El gran libro de la astrología.** Barcelona:
Círculo de Lectores, 1980. 256p. $C.
Translation of **The Compleat Astrologer,** a pictorial
encyclopedia describing astrology and its influence on civilization.

133.6—Palmistry

*Benavides, Rodolfo. **La verdad está en las manos.** México:
Mexicanos Unidos, 1979. 469p. $D.
A general treatment of palmistry by one of Mexico's most
popular authors.

Hutchinson, Beryl. **Su vida en sus manos.** Madrid: EDAF,
1979. 269p. (Plus vitae). $C.

Translation of **Your Life in Your Hands**. Written by a librarian from the International Institute for Psychic Investigation, this book discusses the different aspects of palmistry and their meaning for a person's life.

La quiromancia: el carácter en sus manos. Madrid: Altalena, 1980. 91p. (Maraflash). $E.
A brief introduction to palmistry.

133.82—Telepathy

La telepatía; nuestro sexto sentido. Madrid: Altalena, 1980. 89p. (Maraflash). $E.
A brief description of telepathy.

133.9013—Personal Survival, Nature of the Spiritual World, and Life after Death

*Iverson, Jeffrey. **¿Más de una vida?** Barcelona: ·Martínez Roca, 1979. 179p. $D.
Translation of **More Lives Than One?** Describes cases of persons who remember past lives under hypnosis.

Moody, Raymond. **Vida después de la vida**. México: EDAF, 1977. 173p. $D.
Translation of **Life after Life**. Case studies of persons who recall their close encounters with death.

135.3—DREAMS

*Cano, Román J. **Los secretos de los sueños**. Barcelona: Martínez Roca, 1983. 156p. (Fontana práctica). $D.
This popular treatment combines both the traditional and the psychological interpretation of dreams.

*Holzer, Hans. **Interpretación práctica de los sueños**. Barcelona: Martínez Roca, 1981. 187p. $D.
A guide to understanding psychic and paranormal dreams.

*El libro supremo de los sueños**. México: Epoca, 1978. 187p. $E.
One of the most popular books on the meaning of dreams. Arranged alphabetically by object, event, or person occurring in the dream.

Llop Sala, Enrique (pseud. Soliatán Sun). **El significado de los sueños.** Barcelona: Martínez Roca, 1979. 176p. (La otra ciencia). $D.
A history of dream interpretation, followed by a dictionary arrangement of symbols and their meanings.

Los sueños: qué significan, cómo interpretarlos. Madrid: Altalena, 1980. 92p. (Maraflash). $D.
A brief but excellent introduction to dream interpretation.

137—GRAPHOLOGY

*Benavides, Rodolfo. **La escritura huella del alma: manual práctico de grafología.** México: Mexicanos Unidos, 1977. 385p. $D.
A guide to graphology written by a popular Mexican author.

Hughes, Albert E. **Lo que revela su escritura.** Madrid: EDAF, 1980. 150p. (Plus vitae). $E.
Translation of **What Your Handwriting Reveals.** A layperson's guide to handwriting analysis.

138—PHYSIOGNOMY

*Durville, Simón. **El espejo de ti mismo.** Barcelona: Martínez Roca, 1981. 271p. $D.
A guide to self-awareness using face and palm reading, graphology and astrology.

Vignes Rouges, Jean. **Tu carácter.** Madrid: Daimón, 1970. 495p. $D.
A guide to judging personalities, with an emphasis on phrenology.

150—PSYCHOLOGY

Davidoff, Linda L. **Introducción a la psicología.** México: McGraw-Hill, 1979. 642p. $B.

Translation of **Introduction to Psychology**. Describes differential and social psychology, schools of thought, and psychological research methods.

*Velázquez, José M. **Manual de psicología elemental**. New York: Minerva, 1979. 160p. $E.
A brief overview of basic psychology.

Vidales, Ismael. **Psicología general**. México: Limusa, 1978. 264p. $D.
General coverage of the concepts of personality, conduct, perception, mental health, tests, and intelligence.

152.4—Emotions and Feelings

Jagot, Paul C. **La timidez vencida**. México: Mexicanos Unidos, 1979. 227p. $E.
Techniques on conquering shyness.

Zimbardo, Philip G. **La timidez: qué es, qué hacer con ella**. Bogotá: Fondo Educativo Interamericano, 1979. 304p.
Translation of **Shyness**. The most complete book for the layperson on overcoming shyness.

153.14—Mnemonic Systems

*Brothers, Joyce. **Diez días para obtener una memoria sorprendente**. México: Herrero, 1980. 246p. $D.
Translation of **Ten Days to a Successful Memory**. The very popular Dr. Brothers, who has had Spanish media exposure, describes how to improve the memory.

154.63—Dreams

*Freud, Sigmund. **La interpretación de los sueños**. Madrid: Alianza, 1979. 3v. $B.
The classic psychological study on dreams. Very popular in Spanish.

154.7—Hypnotism

*Jagot, Paul C. **Hipnotismo, magnetismo y sugestión**. Barcelona: Iberia, 1982. 396p. $D.
Techniques and applications of hypnotism, animal magne-

tism, and mental suggestion by a popular author. Also published by Editores Mexicanos Unidos.

155—DIFFERENTIAL PSYCHOLOGY

Bachs, Jordi. **Psicología diferencial**. Barcelona: CEAC, 1980. 189p. $D.
Covers the psychological differences caused between individuals by environment, inheritance, race, sex, culture, and family.

155.4—CHILD PSYCHOLOGY

Bas, Margarite. **Padres jóvenes, hijos pequeños**. 2. ed. León, España: Everest, 1980. 223p. (Padres e Hijos). $E.
A basic easy-to-read book on factors that influence a child's education. Focuses on the parent's role as primary educator.

Bierge, José. **Cuidado y educación de los hijos**. Barcelona: CEAC, 1976. 178p. (Nueva enciclopedia femenina). $D.
A well-illustrated book on child development from birth to pre-puberty, chronologically arranged by age.

Brazelton, T. Berry. **Niños y madres: los primeros doce meses**. Bogotá: Carlos Valencia, 1979. 363p. $B.
Translation of **Infants and Mothers**. A noted expert on child psychology describes the first 12 months of a child's life.

Gordon, Thomas. **P.E.T., padres eficáz y técnicamente preparados**. México: Diana, 1978. 307p. $D.
Translation of **P.E.T., Parent Effectiveness Training**. Stresses how to improve communication between parent and child.

*Lehmann, Peter G. **De cero a catorce años: consejos para una educación moderna**. 2. ed. León, Espanña: Everest, 1979. 192p. $E.
Advice for parents on how to deal with common problems

experienced by children from birth to 14 years of age. Arranged chronologically.

*Snijders-Oomen, N. **Psicología para la educación del niño: psicología infantil práctica para padres y educadores.** Bilbao: Mensajero, 1979. 175p. $E.
A book of general child psychology with advice for parents and teachers on how to help a child become a well-rounded person.

*Tau, Mario. **El ABC de la psicología infantil.** Barcelona: Bruguera, 1980. 219p. (Libro práctico). $E.
This basic, easy-to-read, child psychology book describes development in general and offers advice on common problems such as children and divorce, shyness, lying, and bedwetting.

Wolman, Benjamin. **El niño ante el temor, el miedo y el terror.** México: Lasser Press Mexicana, 1981. 191p. $D.
Translation of **Children's Fears.** Written specifically for parents. The first part of the book describes the psychology of children's fears during certain developmental stages, and the second discusses individual fears, such as the fear of animals, fear of the dark, etc., and how parents can help children overcome them.

155.5—PSYCHOLOGY OF ADOLESCENTS

Castillo Ceballos, Gerardo. **Los adolescentes y sus problemas.** Pamplona: EUNSA, 1980. 232p. (Educación NT). $D.
An aid for parents and teachers who want to better understand teenagers and help them in the maturation process.

157.7—DISORDERS OF CHARACTER AND PERSONALITY

Schreiber, Flora Rheta. **Sybil.** Barcelona: Pomaire, 1977. 502p. $E.
The life story of a woman with multiple personalities.

158—APPLIED PSYCHOLOGY

*Carnegie, Dale. **Cómo ganar amigos e influir sobre las personas.** Buenos Aires: Sudamericana, 1980. 249p. $D.
Translation of **How to Win Friends and Influence People.**
International bestseller on human relations in business and in social contacts. Also published by Edhasa.

*Carnegie, Dale. **Cómo suprimir las preocupaciones y disfrutar de la vida.** Buenos Aires: Sudamericana, 1978. 289p. $D.
Translation of **How to Stop Worrying and Start Living.** A practical and inspiring book on conquering worry.

*Dyer, Wayne W. **Tus zonas erróneas.** Barcelona: Grijalbo, 1980. 321p. $D.
Translation of **Your Erroneous Zones.** Advice on attaining self-actualization.

*Hill, Napoleón. **Piense y hágase rico.** Barcelona: Bruguera, 1975. 331p. (Libro Práctico). $E.
Translation of **Think and Grow Rich.** Philosophy and formulas for financial success and spiritual satisfaction.

*Maltz, Maxwell. **Psico–cibernética; nuevo método para la conquista de una vida más fecunda y dichosa.** México: Herrero, 1977. 315p. $D.
Translation of **Psycho–cybernetics.** Emphasizes self image as the key to a successful life.

*Mandino, Og. **El vendedor más grande del mundo.** México: Diana, 1975. 123p. $E.
Translation of **The Greatest Salesman in the World.** How to sell oneself to others and achieve success.

*Peale, Norman Vincent. **El poder del pensamiento tenáz.** Barcelona: Grijalbo, 1965. 286p. $D.
Translation of **The Power of Positive Thinking.** Popular guide on how to attain peace of mind and improved health. This is the best read of the author's titles on positive thinking.

*Smith, Manuel. **Cuando digo no, me siento culpable.** Barcelona: Grijalbo, 1977. 438p. $D.
Translation of **When I Say No, I Feel Guilty.** Advice on becoming more assertive.

158.2—Interpersonal Relations

*Berne, Eric. **¿Qué dice Ud después de decir hola?** Barcelona: Grijalbo, 1980. 490p. $D.
Translation of **What Do You Say after You Say Hello?** A good introduction to transactional analysis and its applications.

*Harris, Thomas Anthony. **Yo estoy bien, tú estás bien.** Barcelona: Grijalbo, 1980. 402p. $D.
Translation of **I'm O.K., You're O.K.** Another popular introduction to transactional analysis.

James, Muriel. **Nacidos para triunfar: análisis transaccional con experimentos gestalt.** Bogotá: Fondo Educativo Interamericano, 1976. 270p. $D.
Translation of **Born to Win.** Transactional analysis and its application to daily life.

158.9—Dianetics

*Hubbard, LaFayette Ronald. **Dianética: la ciencia moderna de la salud mental.** México: Publicaciones Dianéticas, 1978. 425p. $E.
Translation of **Dianetics.** Mental health practices for individuals, families, and groups. Publicity through the Spanish-language media has made this a much requested title.

160—LOGIC

*García-Tuduri, Rosaura. **Lógica.** New York: Minerva, 1966. 206p.
A concise and easy-to-read introduction to logic. Includes bibliographies for further reading.

170—ETHICS (MORAL PHILOSOPHY)

*Lin, Yutang. **La importancia de vivir.** Buenos Aires: Sudamericana, 1982. 457p. $D.
A much requested title that interprets the Chinese philosophy of life and contrasts it with Western thought.

Veatch, Henry Babcock. **Etica del ser racional.** Barcelona: Labor, 1972. 176p. (Nueva colección Labor). $E.
Translation of **Rational Man.** An excellent introduction to ethics.

184—PLATONIC PHILOSOPHY

Plato. **Diálogos.** México: Porrúa, 1979. 785p. (Sépan cuantos). $D.
Contains the most important dialogues, including the Apology, Gorgias, Crito, The Republic, Meno, Parmenides, The Sophist, and Timaeus. The introduction discusses the dialogues and their importance in the development of Platonic thought.

193—GERMAN PHILOSOPHY

Nietzsche, Friedrich Wilhelm. **Así habló Zaratustra.** Madrid: Alianza, 1980. 472p. $D.
Translation of **Thus Spoke Zarathustra.** The author calls on people to examine their traditional values and suggests that religion has lost its meaning and power. Also published by Editores Mexicanos Unidos.

196—SPANISH PHILOSOPHY

Unamuno Jugo, Miguel de. **Del sentimiento trágico de la vida.** Madrid: Espasa Calpe, 1980. 272p. (Colección Austral). $E.
Addresses the tragedy of life, in which reason is not enough yet faith is utterly irrational.

200 Religion

200.1—PHILOSOPHY AND THEORY

Fierro, Alfredo. **El hecho religioso.** Barcelona: Salvat,
    1981. 64p. (Temas clave). $E.
A well-illustrated, objective introduction to religion,
its components, its place in society and its scientific
study.

220.2—BIBLE CONCORDANCES

Denyer, Carlos P. **Concordancia de las Sagradas Escrituras.**
    Miami: Caribe, 1969. 936p. $A.
A concordance of the Bible with an emphasis on Roman
Catholicism up to the Reformation.

220.561—Spanish Language Bibles

La Biblia al día: paráfrasis. Wheaton, Ill.: Living Bibles,
    n.d. 267p. $E.
A translation of **The Living Bible, Paraphrased.**
Simplified text aids in understanding the Bible.

La Biblia de Jerusalén. Bilbao: Desclée de Brouwer, 1979.
    864p. (Edición popular). $E.

14

The **Jerusalem Bible**. A non-denominational Bible approved by the Roman Catholic Church.

La Biblia nueva Latinoamericana. Madrid: Ediciones Paulinas, 1981. 471p. (Edición Pastoral). $C.
Illustrated with scenes from everyday Latin American life, including its poverty. For this reason, this Bible was banned in Argentina. Recommended by leaders in the charismatic movement.

*La **sagrada Biblia**. Madrid: Biblioteca de Autores Cristianos, 1979. 1523p. (Nacar-Colunga edition). HB. $C.
This is the Standard Roman Catholic Bible.

*La **santa Biblia: antiguo y nuevo testamento/antigua versión de Casiodoro Reina (1569), revisada por Cipriano de Valera (1602)**. Miami: Vida, 1980. 951p. (Edición especial con letra grande). HB. $A.
The Reina-Valera edition is comparable to the King James version in English and is the most used Protestant Bible. Large type edition.

*La **santa Biblia: antiguo y nuevo testamento/antigua versión de Casiodoro Reina (1569), revisada por Cipriano de Valera (1602)**. New York: Amer. Bible Society, 1980. 951p. $D.
The standard Protestant Bible in Spanish.

220.6—Bible Interpretation

Charpentier, Etienne. **Para leer el Antiguo Testamento**. Navarra, Spain: Verbo Divino, 1983. 122p. $A.
An aid to reading and understanding the Old Testament from a Catholic point of view. **Para leer el Nuevo Testamento** by the same author and publisher covers the New Testament.

Miles, A.R. **Introducción popular al estudio de las sagradas escrituras**. Miami: Caribe, n.d. 234p.
An introductory study of the Bible from a Protestant viewpoint.

220.9—Bible, Geography, and History

Barthel, Manfred. **Lo que dijo verdaderamente la Biblia**. Barcelona: Martínez Roca, 1982. (Nueva fontana). $D.

A well-documented look at Biblical myths and their origins. Discusses the Bible from a historical perspective. Of interest to both believers and non-believers.

Enciclopedia de la Biblia. Navarra, Spain: Verbo Divino, 1983. 326p. HB. $E.
Translation of **The Lion Encyclopedia of the Bible.** A beautifully illustrated introduction to the Bible describing the daily life, political history, and geography at the time of the Scriptures.

232.9—JESUS CHRIST

Martínez Cajal, Jesús. **La verdad sobre Jesucristo: su biografía narrada por quienes le conocieron.** Barcelona: Sopena, 1976. 478p. (Biblioteca Hispania Ilustrada). HB. $C.
The life of Christ as told in the Bible, with commentaries.

242—DEVOTIONAL LITERATURE

Augustine, Saint. **Confesiones.** México: Porrúa, 1970. 258p. (Sépan cuantos). $D.
A historical work that is occasionally requested.

Francesco D'Assisi, Saint. **Florecillas de San Francisco de Asís.** México: Porrúa, 1977. 304p. (Sépan cuantos). $C.
Meditative anecdotes from the life of Saint Francis.

*Imitatio Christi. **Imitación de Cristo por Tomás de Kempis.** México: Porrúa, 1978. 198p. (Sépan cuantos). $D.
A devotional classic originally written in the 1500s.

*Teresa, Saint. **Las moradas: libro de su vida.** México: Porrúa, 1972. 314p. (Sépan cuantos). $D.
Traces the development of prayer and also tells St. Teresa's life story. One of the classics of mysticism.

264.02—ROMAN CATHOLIC PUBLIC WORSHIP

Flóres M., Francisco. **Devocionario popular.** Guadalajara:
Ateneo Sacerdotal, 1983. $E.
Contains common prayers and the ordinary of the Mass.

282.092—SAINTS

Butler, Alban. **Vidas de los santos de Butler.** México:
Clute, 1969. 4v. HB. $A.
Translation of **Lives of the Saints.** Considered the most
comprehensive work in Spanish on the saints.

Ordoñez, Valeriano. **Los santos, noticia diaria.** Barcelona:
Herder, 1980. 50p. $D.
Biographical sketches of saints, arranged chronolog-
ically by day of the year.

*Vann P., Joseph. **Vidas de Santos.** Barcelona: Grijalbo,
1974. 435p. (Colección Biografías Gandesa). HB. $D.
Translation of **Lives of Saints.** Contains a selection of
the most popular saints. Each biography is several pages
long.

289—OTHER SECTS

*Carmona, Blas. **Profetas sospechosos, sectas de ayer y de
hoy.** Barcelona: Gedia, 1980. 127p. $E.
Objectively describes the origins and beliefs of
religious sects, such as the Masons, the Jehovah's Wit-
nesses, and the Theosophical Society.

290—COMPARATIVE RELIGION

*Cid Priego, Carlos. **Historia de las religiones.** Barcelona: Sopena, 1972. 738p. (Biblioteca Hispania Ilustrada). HB. $C.
The history of world religions from prehistoric times to

the 1960s, with an emphasis on Roman Catholicism up to the Reformation.

Tokarev, Sergei Aleksandrovich. **Historia de las religiones.** Madrid: Akal, 1979. 530p. (Akal bolsillo). $D.
This somewhat scholarly work by a Marxist outlines the development of religion from the earliest times to the present. Emphasizes religion's role in society and discusses several religions not covered in other Spanish titles.

292—MYTHOLOGY

*Garibay Kintana, Angel María. **Mitología griega: dioses y héroes.** México: Porrúa, 1977. 260p. $D.
Brief descriptions of gods and heroes from Greek mythology. Alphabetically arranged.

Gaytan, Carlos. **Diccionario mitológico.** México: Diana, 1975. 239p. (Colección moderna). $D.
A dictionary of universal mythology.

Rodriguez Adrados, Jesús V. **Dioses y héroes, mitos clásicos.** Barcelona: Salvat, 1980. 64p. (Temas clave). $E.
Briefly relates the best-known stories of mythology and discusses why ancient myths are still important in our culture.

294—RELIGIONS OF EAST AND SOUTHEAST ASIAN ORIGIN

Parrinder, Edward. **Religiones de Asia.** México: Diana, 1980. 187p. $E.
Translation of **Asian Religions.** Covers the history and beliefs of religion in Asia.

297.122—KORAN

Koran. **El Corán.** Barcelona: Plaza & Janés, 1980. 588p. $D.
One of several editions of this occasionally requested classic.

300 Social Sciences

Ebert, Alan. **Hablan los homosexuales**. Barcelona: Martínez
    Roca, n.d. 395p. $D.
    Translation of **The Homosexuals**. Verbatim interviews
Ebert conducted with 16 gay men.

Horton, Paul B., and Chester L. Hunt. **Sociología**. Méxi-
    co: McGraw-Hill, 1977. 420p.
    Translation of **Sociology**. Introductory textbook on
sociology.

*Lewis, Oscar. **Los hijos de Sánchez: autobiografía de una
    familia mexicana**. 15. ed. México: Mortiz, 1977. 521p.
    $E.
    Translation of **The Children of Sánchez**. The classic
study on the nature of poverty.

Salguero, Miguel (pseud. of Miguel Zuñiga Díaz). **Así vi-
    vimos los Ticos**. San José, Costa Rica: Universitaria
    Centroamericana, 1976. 395p.
    Remarkable journalistic report on the thoughts and
feelings of the people of Costa Rica.

306.89—SEPARATION AND DIVORCE

*Gettleman, Susan, and Janet Markowitz. **El valor de divorciarse.** México: Diana, 1979. 280p. $D.
Translation of **The Courage to Divorce.** A survey of society-created obstacles to divorce, and how to overcome them.

Krantzler, Mel. **Divorcio creador: una nueva oportunidad para el crecimiento personal.** México: Extemporáneos, 1975. 309p. (Colección El viento cambia). $C.
Translation of **Creative Divorce.** Offers the newly divorced person a positive view of the future.

Rivera West, Jorge. **Divorcio feliz.** Madrid: Altalena, 1982. 163p. (Frente a frente). $C.
Designed to help those contemplating divorce. Suggests that divorce can be a positive alternative to continuing an unhappy marriage.

320.473—STRUCTURE, FUNCTIONS, ACTIVITIES OF GOVERNMENT

Machiavelli, Niccolo. **El príncipe.** México: Porrúa, 1970. 53p. $E.
Translation of Machiavelli's **The Prince.** The masterwork on power politics.

*Roy, Joaquín. **El gobierno y los presidentes de los Estados Unidos de América.** Northbrook, Ill.: Quality Books, 1980. 89p. $D.
Contains biographical sketches of the U.S. presidents from Washington to Carter, a list of important dates, and the U.S. Constitution. Very useful for those studying for the citizenship examination.

323—Citizenship and Related Topics

*Hennessey, Denis Lawrence. **Veinticinco lecciones de ciudadanía.** Berkeley: D. L. Lawrence, 1978. 91p. $E.
Spanish edition of **Twenty-five Lessons in Citizenship.** Describes the functions of government and gives important historical background. Includes procedures for obtaining citizenship and sample questions.

*Newhouse, Dora. **Ciudadanía/Citizenship.** Los Angeles: Newhouse, 1977. 136p. $E.
A bilingual edition with sample questions on American history and government.

330—ECONOMICS

Samuelson, Paul Anthony. **Curso de economía moderna.** Madrid: Aguilar, 1979. $A.
A basic textbook used in many U.S. universities.

Singer, Leslie. **Economía simplificada.** México: General, 1977. 207p.
Translation of **Economics Made Simple.** The principles of economics for the layperson.

340.03—LAW DICTIONARIES

*Robb, Louis A. **Diccionario de términos legales/ Dictionary of Legal Terms.** México: Limusa, 1980. $D.
A dictionary of equivalent English and Spanish terms used in the field of law.

342.083—CITIZENSHIP AND NATIONALITY

*Ades, Daniel. **Cómo obtener su residencia legal en los Estados Unidos de América y evitar problemas de inmigración.** Publicaciones Latinas, 1982. 106p. $E.
Gives advice for immigrating legally by becoming part of the mainstream, such as learning English and establishing good credit. Also explains immigration laws and lists helpful agencies.

*Tirado, Arturo R. **Fácil inmigración a los Estados Unidos.** Orbe, 1981. 123p. $D.
Describes the procedures for immigrating legally to the United States, with emphasis on special visas, work permits, necessary documents, social security, deportation, and filing of income tax.

*Williams, Rod. **Cómo inmigrar sin abogado.** Los Alamitos,
Calif.: 1981. 99p. $C.
Outlines procedures for legally immigrating to the U-
nited States, without legal assistance. Includes forms and
instructions for their completion.

351.7—ESPIONAGE

Borosage, Robert L. **Los archivos de la C.I.A.** México:
Diana, 1980. 300p. $D.
Translation of **The C.I.A. File.** The origins and activi-
ties of the CIA.

362.29—ADDICTIONS

Jaffe, Jerome. **Vicios y drogas: problemas y soluciones.**
México: Harper & Row, 1980. 128p. (La psicología y
tú). $D.
Translation of **Addictions,** a part of the Life Cycle
series. Describes different addictions, their causes,
effects, and cures. Objectively examines drug use in many
cultures.

362.292—Alcoholism

North, Robert. **El alcoholismo en la juventud.** México:
Pax-México, 1980. $E.
Translation of **Teenage Drinking.** Explains why teenagers
drink and suggests what to do about it.

362.293—Drug Addiction

Freiza, F. **El fenómeno droga.** Barcelona: Salvat, 1982.
64p. (Temas clave). $E.
Describes the history and uses of drugs, and the
symptoms, prevention, and cure of drug abuse. Includes
common legal drugs such as tobacco, alcohol, pain killers,
and over-the-counter drugs, as well as illegal drugs such as
cocaine, opium, and heroin. Also discusses world-wide
social problems caused by drug traffic.

*Sotelo Regil, Luis F. **Drogadicción juvenil: cómo preve-nirla y cómo remediarla.** México: Diana, 1976. 127p. $E.

A handy, easy-to-read guide for parents. Describes drugs and their effects, warning signs, why children turn to drugs, and how to stop them from taking drugs.

362.7044—CHILD ABUSE

*Chase, Naomi Feigelson. **Un niño ha sido golpeado: la vio-lencia contra los niños, una tragedia moderna.** México: Diana, 1979. 265p. $D.

Translation of **A Child is Being Beaten.** Overview of the history of child abuse, children's rights, the origin of the problem, and the rehabilitation of parents and children. Includes sample case studies.

Kempe, Ruth S. **Niños maltratados.** Madrid: Morata, 1979. 230p. (Serie Bruner). $D.

Translation of **Child Abuse.** A discussion of the nature of child abuse, its forms and origins, and current efforts to help the victims. A compassionate, well-written book on a difficult subject.

365.9882—PENAL INSTITUTIONS IN FRENCH GUIANA

*Charriere, Henri. **Papillón.** Barcelona: Círculo de Lectores, 1972. 552p. $D.

This Frenchman's adventures in escaping from Devil's Island are still very popular in Spanish. **Banco** is the sequel.

366—FREEMASONRY

*Martínez Zaladua, Ramón. **Historia de la masonería en His-pano-américa.** México: Costa-Amic, 1980. 181p. $D.

An account of the Masons' influence in Hispanic America.

371.3—PERSONAL EDUCATION

*Hernández Santiago, René G. **El éxito en tus estudios.** México: Trillas, 1980. 134p. $E.
Suggests how students can develop and improve study skills and habits. Includes techniques on library research.

Preparación para el exámen de equivalencia de la escuela superior (en español). New York: Arco, 1981. 352p. $D.
Translation of **High School Equivalency Diploma Tests.** Reviews the five areas covered in the test.

371.9—SPECIAL EDUCATION

Petit, Jean. **La educación de niños deficientes.** Madrid: Magisterio Español, 1971. 357p. (Biblioteca de ciencias de la educación). $D.
A guide for educators of deaf, blind, physically disabled, and mentally retarded children. Parents will also find much valuable information here.

371.914—Students with Linguistic Handicaps

Stengl, Ingebury. **Los problemas de lenguaje en el niño: reconocimiento precóz y corrección.** Barcelona: Fontanella, 1978. 165p. (Educación). $D.
Helps parents recognize their children's speech problems, and suggests exercises to alleviate them.

*Wagner, Rudolf. **La dislexia y su hijo.** México: Diana, 1979. 152p. $D.
Describes dyslexia and its causes, and suggests exercises to improve this condition.

372.21—PRESCHOOL EDUCATION

*Mayesky, Mary. **Actividades creativas para niños pequeños.** México: Diana, 1978. 241p. $D.
Translation of **Creative Activities for Young Children.** Includes a multitude of activities that will help the child to grow emotionally, physically, and mentally.

Spencer, Zane. **150 juegos y actividades pre-escolares.**
Barcelona: CEAC, 1981. (Colección Educación y
Enseñanza). 179p. $D.
Translation of **150 Plus! Games and Activities for Early
Childhood.** Contains many ideas for holiday and seasonal
activities.

372.292—Montessori System

*Hainstock, Elizabeth G. **Enseñanza Montessori en el hogar:
los años preescolares.** México: Diana, 1975. 126p. HB.
$D.
Translation of **Teaching Montessori in the Home: The Pre-
school Years.** Introduces parents to the Montessori method,
and suggests specific exercises to develop the senses, language, coordination, realistic thinking, and order sequence.
Shows how to understand a child and apply self-paced learning.

*Hainstock, Elizabeth G. **Enseñanza Montessori en el hogar:
los años escolares.** México: Diana, 1978. 186p. $D.
Translation of **Teaching Montessori in the Home: The
School Years.** Presents math and language development
exercises for individual study or study with parental help.

395—ETIQUETTE

*Carreño, Manuel Antonio. **Manual de urbanidad y buenas
maneras: de consulta indispensable para niños, jóvenes y
adultos.** Virginia Gardens, Fla.: América, n.d. 432p.
$E.
Originally written in the 1800s, this classic reveals
the gracious conduct of an earlier time. It is still requested and read. Contains an updated section on the most
requested subjects: gift giving, weddings, and table setting.

*Vanderbilt, Amy. **Etiqueta cotidiana de Amy Vanderbilt.**
México: Diana, 1981. 262p. $E.
Translation of the 1970 edition of Amy Vanderbilt's
Everyday Etiquette. While some of the information is out of
date, this is the only title in Spanish on American
etiquette.

398—FOLKLORE

Rael, Juan B. **Cuentos españoles de Colorado y Nuevo México.**
    Santa Fé: Museum of New Mexico, 1977.
    A compilation of folktales from Colorado and New Mexico.
Arranged by theme.

398.2—Legends

Alegría, Ciro. **Panki y el guerrero.** Lima: Industrial Grá-
    fica, 1968. 95p.
    Collection of 16 legends from the Amazon region, the
Peruvian Andes, Chile, Brazil, Mexico, and Colombia.

Armellada, Fray Cesáreo de. **Panton . . . (Una mano de cu-
    entos de los indios pemón).** Caracas: Consucre, 1979.
    54p.
    Five legends of the Pemón Indians of Venezuela.

Asturias, Miguel Angel. **Leyendas de Guatemala.** Buenos
    Aires: Losada, 1957. 150p.
    Collection of six Guatemalan legends and two essays
written by the winner of the 1967 Nobel Prize in literature.

*Blackmore, Vivien. **El maíz tiene color de oro: leyendas
    vegetales.** Illustrated by Susana Martínez-Ostos. Mé-
    xico: Novaro, 1981. 48p.
    Beautiful collection of six pre-Columbian Mexican
legends about plants, flowers, and fruits.

Campos Menéndez, Enrique. **Sólo el viento.** Santiago: Ga-
    briela Mistral, 1973. 158p.
    Remarkable collection of 12 Chilean legends of ancient
Ona origin (an extinct pre-Columbian Indian race that
inhabited Tierra del Fuego until the late 1800s).

Cok de Leonard, Carmen. **Los gemelos contra los gigantes.**
    Illustrated by the author. México: Valle de México,
    1980. 70p.
    This story, taken from the great Mayan manuscript "Popol
Vuh," tells how two twin brothers fought the giants who
controlled the earth and thus prepared the earth for future
men and women.

*Coll y Toste, Cayetano. **Leyendas puertorriqueñas.** Méxi-
    co: Orión, 1974. 202p.
    By a Puerto Rican author of the late 1800s who wrote the
legends of his country in a simple, direct style.

Garrido de Rodríguez, Neli. **Leyendas Argentinas.** Illustrated by José Miguel Heredia. Buenos Aires: Plus Ultra, 1981. 111p.
Delightful collection of short, pre-Columbian legends of South America.

*González Casanova, Pablo. **Cuentos indígenas.** México: UNAM, 1965. 160p.
Excellent collection of short, pre-Columbian Mexican legends of animals. The Nahuatl version of each legend is written on one side of each page, and the author's Spanish translation is written on the other side.

*Hinojosa, Francisco. **La vieja que comía gente: leyendas de espantos.** Illustrated by Leonel Maciel. México: Novaro, 1981. 48p.
Four Mexican legends of spirits and phantoms. Includes spectacular color illustrations.

*Hinojosa, Francisco, and Raúl Navarrete. **El sol, la luna y las estrellas: leyendas de la creación.** Illustrated by Francisco Toledo. México: Novaro, 1981. 48p.
Four pre-Columbian Mexican legends that describe the creation of the earth.

*Jordana Laguna, José Luis. **Leyendas amazónicas.** Madrid: Doncel, 1976. 138p. $E.
Excellent collection of 21 Peruvian legends of the Amazon region.

*Kortycz, Marcos, and Ana García Kobeh. **De tigres y tlacuaches: leyendas animales.** México: Novaro, 1981. 46p.
Delightful adaptation of six Mexican legends about animals that will charm readers with their wit and resourcefulness.

Leal de Noguera, María. **Cuentos viejos.** 5. ed. Illustrated by Osvaldo Salas. San José, Costa Rica: Editorial Costa Rica, 1981. 171p.
A well-known collection of 24 traditional tales from Costa Rica. Originally published in 1938.

*Martínez, Paulina and others. **Leyendas argentinas.** Illustrated by Csecs. Buenos Aires: Sigmar, 1977. 60p.
Collection of 37 folk tales and legends from various Argentinian provinces.

Movsichoff Zavala, Paulina. **El cóndor de la vertiente: le-

yenda salasaca. Illustrated by Oswaldo Viteri. Quito: Ediciones del Sol, 1978. 24p.
Pre-Columbian legend from Ecuador that tells how a condor loved and protected the Salasaca people.

*Murillo, José. **Leyendas para todos.** Buenos Aires: Guadalupe, 1978. 143p.
A collection of eight fascinating, original legends from South America.

*Palma, Ricardo. **Tradiciones peruanas.** Madrid: Aguilar, 1962. 98p.
Brief essays with small, simple illustrations of life during Inca times. Also covers the Conquest, and colonial and modern Peru.

*Samaniego, Felix María. **Fábulas.** Barcelona: Verón, 1972. 170p. $E.
Fascinating collection of famous 18th century fables. Should charm all Spanish-speakers.

Soler Blanch, Carmen. **Leyendas incas.** Barcelona: Instituto de Artes Gráficas, 1964. 194p.
Outstanding collection of 46 legends illustrating the rich oral tradition of the pre-Columbian Incas, which was recorded by the Spaniards.

398.961—Spanish Proverbs

Iribarren Rodríguez, José. **Repertorio de modismos y frases proverbiales (El por qué de los dichos).** Madrid: Aguilar, 1974. 780p. $C.
Spanish idiomatic expressions, popular sayings, and proverbs--their meaning and origin.

400 Languages

425—GRAMMAR

*Añorga Larralde, Joaquín. **Gramática bilingüe: inglés-español, español-inglés.** New York: Minerva, 1972. 256p. $E.

Presents and explains English and Spanish grammar, and compares each. The first part of the book is for students of English, and the second part is for students of Spanish.

425.8—English Language Verbs

*Craig, Ruth Parle. **Diccionario de 201 verbos ingleses.** Woodbury, N.Y.: Barron's, 1972. 432p. $D.

A useful reference dictionary of commonly used English verbs completely conjugated. Gives their idiomatic usage.

428.2—ENGLISH LANGUAGE

Barnet, William. **Aprenda inglés sin maestro.** México: Mexicanos Unidos, 1977. 153p. $D.

The emphasis is on pronunciation and vocabulary improvement in English. There are a few typographical and spelling errors, but for the most part the information is correct.

29

*Berlitz Schools. **El Berlitz sin maestro, inglés.** New York: Grosset, 1951. 251p. HB. $D.
Contains 38 lessons of increasing difficulty on how to improve conversation. Includes a pronunciation guide.

*Cortina, Rafael Díez de la. **Método Cortina inglés en 20 lecciones.** New York: R. D. Cortina, 1977. 374p. HB. $D.
The most complete book on learning English. Contains a grammar with clear explanations, conversation lessons, pronunciation guide and a bilingual dictionary.

Dixson, Robert. **Curso completo de inglés.** New York: Regents, 1973. 4v. $D.
Emphasizes the conversational structures and the vocabulary of everyday American English.

Fernández Gandia, J. **Inglés sin maestro al alcance de todos.** México: Libro-Mex, 1977. 184p. $D.
Contains English grammar exercises for practicing conversation, a pronunciation guide in American English, and aids for improving vocabulary.

*Garza Bores, Jaime. **Construya en inglés.** México: Diana, 1967. 190p. $E.
Explains how to construct sentences by repeating basic English sentence patterns and using them with different words to express different ideas.

Garza Bores, Jaime. **Diviértase aprendiendo inglés.** México: Diana, 1979. 222p. $E.
The emphasis is on sentence construction. Contains more than 40 American songs, with vocabulary and observations concerning the grammatical construction of the lyrics.

Garza Bores, Jaime. **Exprésalo todo en inglés.** México: Diana 1970. 190p. $E.
The first part contains sentence building using the present, past and future tenses of the verb "to be" and sentence patterns. The second part includes conversation.

Garza Bores, Jaime. **Inglés extractado.** México: Diana, 1961. 153p. $E.
Illustrates sentence construction with auxiliary verbs, and gives examples of the differences between English and Spanish verb forms.

*Ghio, Augusto. **Inglés básico.** Madrid: Rodas, 1971. 272p. $E.

Over three million copies of this book have been sold.
It teaches basic English with 850 words and 16 verbs.
Includes a pronunciation guide.

Newman, Laura. **Bienvenido a mi mundo.** Laura Newman, 1980.
202p. $E.
For practicing conversation and improving vocabulary.
Mostly for classroom use. Contains a pronunciation guide.

Whitehouse, Robert. **Inglés práctico sin maestro.** New York:
Regents, 1972. 196p. $E.
Each lesson covers a part of English grammar and includes a section on vocabulary and an exercise with answers
in the back of the book. No pronunciation guide. Also
available on records.

461—WRITTEN AND SPOKEN CODES OF STANDARD SPANISH

*Perera, Hilda. **Acentuación y puntuación.** New York:
Minerva, 1975. 144p. $E.
Guide to punctuation and accents in Spanish.

463—SPANISH LANGUAGE DICTIONARIES

Aristos diccionario ilustrado de la lengua española. Barcelona: Sopena, 1980. 664p. HB. $D.
An especially popular dictionary because of its illustrations and diverse information, such as spelling rules,
units of measurement, coats of arms, grammar, periodic table
of the elements, etc.

Corominas, Joan. **Breve diccionario etimológico de la lengua
castellana.** Madrid: Gredos, 1976. 628p. $D.
A concise, general dictionary of the Spanish language.

**Diccionario iter ortográfico de la lengua castellana, Re-
visado, ampliado y puesto al día; contiene 80.000
palabras, normas ortográficas, conjugación de los
verbos irregulares, paradigmas de los verbos regulares.**
Barcelona: Sopena, 1979. 636p. D.
This orthographic dictionary contains 80,000 words,
orthographic rules, conjugations of irregular verbs, and
paradigms of regular verbs.

*Raluy Poudevida, Antonio. **Diccionario Porrúa de la lengua española.** México: Porrúa, 1980. 848p. $D.
One of the most complete Spanish dictionaries in paperback.

*Vox, **Diccionario general ilustrado de la lengua española.** Barcelona: Bibliograf, 1980. 1780p. HB. $A.
One of the best general purpose Spanish dictionaries. Especially strong on Latin American and Indian terms. Useful for students of Spanish literature and people in need of current usage rules. The illustrations help define terms.

463.1—Specialized Dictionaries

Corripio, Fernando. **Diccionario de incorrecciones, dudas y normas gramaticales.** Barcelona: Bruguera, 1975. 655p. HB. $D.
A dictionary arrangement of Spanish words commonly used in error and correct Anglicisms. Includes a list of standard abbreviations.

Sáinz de Robles, Federico Carlos. **Diccionario español de sinónimos y antónimos.** Madrid: Aguilar, 1980. 1148p. HB. $A.
One of the most comprehensive dictionaries of synonyms and antonyms in Spanish.

*Savainao, Eugene. **Two Thousand and One Spanish and English Idioms.** New York: Barron's, 1976. 677p. $E.
Commonly used Spanish and English idioms, with sample sentences.

463.21—Bilingual Spanish/English–English/Spanish Dictionaries

*Castillo, Carlos, and Otto F. Bond, comps. **The University of Chicago Spanish Dictionary.** Chicago: Univ. of Chicago Pr., 1977. 243p. $D.
A Spanish/English–English/Spanish dictionary with special indication of Spanish American usage and a great variety of idiomatic expressions. Includes information about the language and its regional differences.

Diccionario inglés. Boston: Houghton Mifflin, 1982. 544p. $D.

Contains definitions of English words in both English and Spanish.

*Parnwell, E.C. **Oxford Picture Dictionary of American English English-Spanish edition.** New York: Oxford Univ. Pr., 1978. 77p. $E.
Color illustrations are captioned in both English and Spanish. Very useful for all ages.

*Simon & Schuster's International Dictionary English-Spanish, Spanish-English.** New York: Simon & Schuster, 1973. 1605p. HB. $A.
The best bilingual dictionary in that it has easy-to-read type, technical and scientific terms, new words, terms used in both Latin America and the United States, many examples of usage, and the most idioms of any dictionary of this type.

*University of Chicago Spanish Dictionary: A New Concise Spanish-English and English-Spanish Dictionary of Words and Phrases Basic to the Written and Spoken Languages of Today.** Chicago: Univ. of Chicago Pr., 1977. 488p. $E.
The best of the bilingual dictionaries in paperback. It is very complete for its size, and includes slang and regional words used in Latin America and the United States.

Velásquez de la Cadena, Mariano. **A New Pronouncing Dictionary of the Spanish and English Languages.** Englewood Cliffs, N.J.: Prentice Hall, 1973. 771p. $C.
A standard dictionary with many useful features.

464—SPANISH-LANGUAGE SYNONYMS

*Canal, Julio de la. **Diccionario de sinónimos e ideas afines.** México: CECSA, 1960. 346p. $D.
A dictionary of synonyms.

Horta Massanes, Joaquín. **Diccionario de sinónimos e ideas afines de la rima.** Madrid: Paraninfo, 1978. 363p. $C.
A complete dictionary of Spanish synonyms and rhymes.

465.8—SPANISH-LANGUAGE VERBS

García Pelayo y Gross, Ramón. **Larousse de la conjugación.**
Paris: Larousse, 1982. 175p. HB. $D.
10,000 Spanish verbs conjugated.

Garza Bores, Jaime. **Manual completo de los verbos
auxiliares y regulares en inglés.** México: Diana, 1961.
206p. $E.
How to learn and use auxiliary and irregular English
verbs.

*Kendris, Christopher. **Dictionary of 500 Spanish Verbs
Fully Conjugated in All Tenses. Alphabetically Ar-
ranged.** Woodbury, N.Y.: Barron's, 1971. 532p. $D.
A guide to conjugating Spanish verbs.

467.972—REGIONAL VARIATIONS OF SPANISH (MEXICO)

Santamaría, Francisco. **Diccionario de Mejicanismos.** México: Porrúa, 1978. 1207p. HB. $A.
Indispensable for looking up words used in Mexico, many
of which are of Indian origin.

467.973—REGIONAL VARIATIONS OF SPANISH (UNITED
STATES)

Arnoch-Calbo, Ernesto. **La lengua española en Estados
Unidos.** Madrid: Oficina de Educación Interamericana,
1980. $D.
The Spanish language in the United States, updated to
include usage since 1970. Covers legislation from 1968 to
1980 about bilingual education.

468.2—SPANISH-LANGUAGE GRAMMAR

Alcina Franch, Juan, and José Manuel Blecua. **Gramática española.** Barcelona: Ariel, 1980. 1274p. $A.

A major reference grammar book, suitably indexed to answer any questions about rules, usage, etc.

*Añorga Larralde, Joaquín. **Conozca su idioma.** New York: Minerva, 1977. 355p. $E.

A much requested grammar, useful for independent study by those who want to improve their Spanish.

Añorga Larralde, Joaquín. **Hable con propiedad y correc- ción.** New York: Minerva, 1968. 159p. $E.

Help for speakers of Spanish in correcting common errors in grammar and vocabulary.

500 Pure Sciences

510—MATHEMATICS

Dolciani, Mary P. **Matemáticas modernas para escuelas secundarias.** México: Cultural, 1968. HB. $B.
A translation of **Modern School Mathematics.** This is a standard high school textbook used in many U.S. schools. It contains a review of arithmetic, plus algebra, geometry, and basic statistics.

Sperling, Abraham. **Matemáticas simplificadas.** México: General, 1964. 189p. $D.
A translation of the well-known **Mathematics Made Simple,** which contains basic arithmetic, algebra, geometry, and trigonometry. Clear explanations and solutions to problems make this an excellent choice for independent study.

Stein, Edwin I. **Repaso matemático bilingüe/refresher mathematics.** Boston: Allyn and Bacon, 1971. 306p. HB. $C.
A bilingual mathematics text.

512—ALGEBRA

*Baldor, Aurelio. **Algebra: con gráficos y 6523 ejercicios y**

problemas con respuestas. Guatemala: Cultural Centroamericana, 1975. 575p. HB. $B.
A much requested high school textbook on algebra.

Dolciani, Mary P. **Algebra moderna: estructura y método.**
México: Cultural, 1977. 2v. HB. $B.
Translation of **Modern Algebra.** Although the Baldor
books are better known in Latin America, many schools in the
United States used the Dolciani books.

Johnson, Richard E. **Algebra.** Bogotá: Fondo Educativo Interamericano, 1980. 613p. HB. $B.
An introductory algebra textbook for college students.

513—ARITHMETIC

*Baldor, Aurelio. **Aritmética práctica: con 7008 ejercicios
y problemas.** Madrid: Cultural Centroamericana, 1977.
639p. HB. $B.
An excellent title on arithmetic, covering addition,
subtraction, division, multiplication, and fractions. Used
throughout the Spanish-speaking world—the United States
included—it is especially good for independent study and is
recommended for civil service exams requiring math.

516—GEOMETRY

*Baldor, Aurelio. **Geometría plana y del espacio.** Madrid:
Cultural Centroamericana, 1977. 423p. HB. $B.
Covers high school geometry and provides an introduction
to trigonometry.

516.3—Analytic Geometry

Steen, Frederick Henry. **Geometría analítica.** México: Publicaciones Cultural, 1975. 350p. $B.
Translation of **Analytic Geometry,** which serves as an
introduction to integral and differential calculus.

520—ASTRONOMY

Asimov, Isaac. **El universo.** Madrid: Alianza, 1980. 424p.
$D.
Translation of **The Universe: From Flat Earth to Quasar,**
published in 1966. Describes the development of humanity's
knowledge of the universe.

*Osman, Tony. **El descubrimiento del universo.** Madrid:
PLESA, 1977. 48p. (El descubrimiento de los museos).
$E.
Translation of **The Discovery of the Universe.** Will ap-
peal to younger readers due to its basic format and content.

Ronan, Colin A. **Los amantes de la astronomía.** Barcelona:
Blume, 1982. 192p. $C.
A translation of **The Practical Astronomer,** a basic
introduction to astronomy for the general public and amateur
star gazers. Includes the latest findings of the Viking,
Pioneer and Voyager space missions.

523.1—UNIVERSE (COSMOLOGY)

Ardley, Neil. **El universo.** Barcelona: Jaimes Libros, 1979.
64p. (Vidorama-El mundo del saber). HB. $C.
Translation of **The Universe.** Covers the history of
astronomy, theories on the origin of the universe, the
telescope and other astronomical instruments, the birth and
development of stars and planets and space exploration.
Well-illustrated, high interest format.

Jastrow, Robert. **Hasta que muera el sol.** Buenos Aires:
Emecé, 1979. 172p. $D.
This translation of **Until the Sun Dies** provides a
fascinating discussion of the origins of the universe and of
life itself.

Kerrod, Robin. **Las estrellas y planetas.** Barcelona:
Fontalba, 1980. 125p. (Guías Fontalba). $D.
An introduction to the stars and the planets.

Velikovsky, Immanuel. **Mundos en colisión.** México: Diana,
1980. 343p. $D.
Translation of **Worlds in Collision.** A controversial
book, refuted by many scientists but still often requested.

530—PHYSICS

Klinger, Fred. ¡La física . . . pero si es muy fácil! Barcelona: Marcombo, 1977. 258p. $C.
A theoretical but accessible approach to physics.

*Sintes Olives, Francisco Faustino. Física general y
aplicada. Barcelona: Sopena, 1975. 652p. (Biblioteca
Hispania Ilustrada). HB. $C.
A readable work for the layperson. Emphasizes the
practical applications of physics.

540—CHEMISTRY

Larrazábal y Fernández, Luis. Química elemental. New York:
Minerva, 1966. 2v. $D.
Provides very basic coverage of chemistry.

*Póstigo, Luis. Química general aplicada. Barcelona: Sope-
na, 1980. 638p. (Biblioteca Hispania Ilustrada). HB.
$C.
The general reader will like this book's readability and
its emphasis on the practical applications of chemistry.

Química. México: Publicaciones Cultural, 1980 (c1971).
595p. $C.
Translation of Chemistry, a basic high school text.

Seese, William S. Curso básico de química. México: El
Manual Moderno, 1979. 258p. (Serie MT). $C.
An advanced chemistry textbook that's often requested by
college students.

549—MINERALOGY

Bariard, Pierre. Enciclopedia de los minerales. Barcelona:
Jaimes Libros, 1979. 122p. (Vidorama-Ocía/Consulta).
HB. $C.
Covers selection of well-known and beautiful minerals.
Brief descriptions are accompanied by color photographs of
natural crystal forms.

40   Pure Sciences

Zim, Herbert Spencer. **Reino mineral.** Barcelona: Daimón
1981. 159p. (Pequeña biblioteca Daimón). $D.
A useful guide for the amateur rock collector in identifying minerals and rocks. Includes a brief description on
the geological formation of rocks.

550—EARTH SCIENCES AND GEOLOGY

Harben, Peter. **La tierra.** Barcelona: Jaimes Libros, 1979.
64p. (Vidorama-El mundo del saber). HB. $C.
Translation of **The Earth.** A well-illustrated, attractive work on the birth and development of the planet and
its geology, climate, and natural resources. Good for
younger readers.

Matthews, William. **Geología simplificada.** México: General,
1968. 200p.
Translation of **Geology Made Simple.** A basic work on the
principles of geology.

551.6—CLIMATOLOGY AND WEATHER

Toharia Cortés, Manuel. **Tiempo y clima.** Barcelona: Salvat,
1981. 64p. (Temas clave). $E.
A well-illustrated book on climate and weather fore-
casting.

572—HUMAN RACES

Panyella, Augusto. **Razas humanas.** Barcelona: Sopena, 1979.
696p. (Biblioteca Hispania Ilustrada). HB. $C.
Very readable general book on physical and cultural
anthropology. Contains sections on each race.

574—BIOLOGY

La ciencia de la vida: un milagro de la naturaleza. Barcelona: Sopena, 1980. 479p. HB. $A.
While this book emphasizes the human body, it also
compares different forms of life, their development, re-
production, nutrition, anatomy, chemical makeup, locomotion,
and genetics. An attractive work, useful as both a high
school text and as a general reader.

*Díaz Cubero, José H. **Introducción a las ciencias bioló-
gicas.** n.p.: M. Fernández, 1980. 239p. $D.
A junior high school level book on biology.

Kimball, John W. **Biología.** Bogotá: Fondo Educativo Interamericano, 1971. 762p. $A.
A basic college textbook translation of **Biology**,
originally published by Addison-Wesley.

574.1—Physiology

Cano, Román J. **Biorritmos: el secreto de nuestros mejores
días.** Barcelona: Martínez Roca, 1980. 283p. (Fontana
práctica). $D.
Explains how to improve life and achieve well-being by
using biorhythms.

575—EVOLUTION

*Darwin, Charles Robert. **El orígen de las especies.** Madrid: EDAF, 1979. 533p. (Biblioteca EDAF de bolsillo).
$E.
Translation of **The Origin of the Species**, the classic
that set forth the theory of evolution.

Fernández Ruíz, Benjamín. **La vida, orígen y evolución.**
Barcelona: Salvat, 1980. 64p. (Temas clave). $E.
A well-illustrated basic, yet stimulating, description
of the theories on the origin and evolution of life.

581.634—MEDICINAL PLANTS

*Alvarez Gonzáles, Pedro. **Yerbas medicinales: como curarse con plantas.** México: Mexicana, 1975. 372p. $E.
A classic Mexican title on medicinal plants. Arranged by common plant name, each entry gives the Latin name, plant description, uses, and methods of preparation. Includes an index of ailments and beneficial plants to use in treating them. Glossary of medical terms used is also included.

Cabrera, Luis. **Plantas curativas de México.** México: Libro Mex, 1981. 384p. $E.
Arranged by common plant name. Gives Latin name, uses, and dosage.

Capo, Nicolás. **Mis observaciones clínicas sobre el limón, el ajo y la cebolla: el limón cura más de 170 enfermedades.** México: Libro Mex, 1976. 96p. $E.
A classic title on the curative aspects of lemon, garlic, and onion.

*Manfred, Leo. **Siete mil recetas botánicas a base de mil trescientas plantas medicinales.** Buenos Aires: Kier, 1977. 668p. $C.
A standard book on medicinal plants. Arranged by common name, and includes indexes of Latin names and ailments.

Manual chino de plantas medicinales. México: Concepto, 1982. 432p. $C.
Translation of the last section of the **Manual of the Barefoot Doctor,** used in the Chinese province of Hunan. Describes each plant, its properties, dosage, and preparation.

Pahlow, Mannfried. **El gran libro de las plantas medicinales.** León, Spain: Everest, 1982. 460p. (Colección tiempo libre). $A.
A well-illustrated reference title that covers 400 medicinal plant species. Describes how to find, prepare, and use them, and discusses the curative effects—as well as any side effects—of both familiar and exotic plants.

594—SEASHELLS

Abbott, Robert Tucker. **Conchas marinas.** Barcelona: Daimón, 1979. 159p. (Pequeña biblioteca Daimón). $D.

Intended for amateur beachcombers, this guide lists shells by generic classification and has numerous photographs to aid identification.

600 Technology
(Applied Sciences)

603—TECHNICAL DICTIONARIES

*Franco Ibeas, F. **Diccionario tecnológico inglés-español.**
Madrid: Alhambra, 1980. 707p. $A.
A very complete, up-to-date, one-volume dictionary of
technical terms in English defined in Spanish. An excellent
first choice, as it covers the fields of electronics, accounting, data processing, and mechanics, among others.

610—MEDICAL SCIENCES

Clark, R.L. **El libro de la salud; una enciclopedia médica
para todos.** México: Continental, 1981. 982p. HB $A.
Translation of **The Book of Health.** This standard
reference work for the layperson describes and prescribes
treatment for almost all health problems and diseases.

Diccionario médico familiar. Madrid: Reader's Digest, 1981.
756p. $A.
Provides well-illustrated, general coverage of health,
physiology, growth and development, and psychology. Contains special sections on care of the bedridden, first aid
care, and newborn care.

*Enciclopedia médica para la familia.** Panamá: América, 1980. 576p. $E.
A handy, inexpensive guide to medical problems and functions of the human body. Written for the layperson.

*Werner, David. **Donde no hay doctor: una guía para los campesinos que viven lejos de los centros médicos.** Palo Alto, Calif.: Fundación Hesperian, 1981. 420p. $D.
Originally written for the rural people of México who do not have access to a doctor, this title is very useful in the U.S. because of the influx of Mexican immigrants. It is easy to understand and refutes many dangerous folk remedies and old wives' tales. A section on medicines and prescription drugs is included. Also published by Pax-México.

610.3—Medical Dictionaries

Diccionario médico ilustrado de Melloni. Barcelona: Reverté, 1983. 598p. $A.
A compilation of 25,000 medical terms with brief descriptions. Useful for its anatomical drawings, illustrations of dysfunctions, and chemical formulas.

*Ruiz Torres, Francisco. **Diccionario de términos médicos inglés–español español–inglés.** Madrid: Alhambra, 1981. 593p. HB. $A.
One of the most complete bilingual dictionaries of medical terms.

610.73—Nursing

Hospital Research and Educational Trust, Chicago. **Enfermería Auxiliar.** México: Nueva Interamericana, 1972. 434p. $A.
Translation of **Being a Nursing Aide.** Offers clear step-by-step procedures for nurse's aides. Also useful to those caring for an ill person at home.

Mayes, Mary E. **Manual para la auxiliar de enfermería.** 3. ed. México: Nueva Interamericana, 1978. 347p. $A.
Translation of **Nurse's Aide Study Manual.** Covers anatomy, patient care, and the responsibility and professional ethics of nursing.

611—HUMAN ANATOMY

*Durfort Coll, M. **El cuerpo humano.** Barcelona: Jover, 1980. 75p. (Colección Natura). HB. Spiralbound. $C.
An attractively illustrated anatomy book for the general public.

Murray, Irwin MacKay. **Anatomía humana simplificada.** México: General, 1971. 178p. $D.
Translation of **Human Anatomy Made Simple.** More detailed than **El cuerpo humano,** but all the illustrations are in black and white.

612—HUMAN PHYSIOLOGY

Dihigo y Llanos, Mario E. **Biología humana; anatomía, fisiología e higiene.** México: Escuela Nueva, 1980. 416p. $D.
A junior high school textbook on human biology, anatomy, physiology, and hygiene.

*Jainin, Robert. **El cuerpo humano, ese desconocido.** Barcelona: Toray, 1980. 154p. HB. $C.
Translated from the French. Similar in style to the television program "The Body Human," this title discusses topics such as the practice of medicine in different cultures and time periods, scientific discoveries, and how the body functions. Excellent for browsing, not meant for reference use.

Ward, Brian. **El cuerpo humano.** Barcelona: Jaimes Libros, 1980. 64p. (El mundo del saber). HB. $C.
Translation of **The Human Body,** part of the British series **The World of Knowledge.** This well-illustrated description of how the body works contains excellent general information younger readers.

612.6—Human Reproduction

*Arnstein, Helen S. **Tu hijo y el sexo.** México: Pax-México, 1973. 162p. $E.
Translation of **Your Growing Child and Sex.** Discusses a child's physical and emotional development through the college years.

*Beers, Laura. **Viva mejor.** Bogotá: Educar, 1983. 304p.
(Su cuerpo). $D.
A well-illustrated, large format paperback describing
the physical and emotional aspects of sex. This edition
combines books previously published separately on health
(**Salud** by Russell Miller), dietetics (**Dietética** by Henry
Ericksen), and beauty (**Belleza**, by Arline Usden).

*Boix, Federico. **¿Papá, cómo nace un niño?** Barcelona: Nova
Terra, 1971. 15p.
Straightforward approach to childbirth, with excellent
illustrations. Simple explanations are given by the father
to a girl and a boy upon the arrival of their new baby
brother. Breast-feeding, birth and affection are effect-
ively explained. Parents can use this book with young
children.

*Boston Women's Health Book Collective. **Nuestros cuerpos
nuestras vidas.** Boston: 1976. 382p. $D.
Translation of **Our Bodies, Ourselves,** with photographs
of Hispanic women.

Comfort, Alex. **The Joy of Sex; guía ilustrada del amor.**
Barcelona: Grijalbo, 1981. 335p. $D.
Translated from the English edition with the same
illustrations, but in a smaller format.

*Domínguez, J. **Felicidad sexual: matrimonial y prematri-
monial.** New York: Plus Ultra Educational, 1971. 346p.
$E.
A popular marriage manual. No illustrations.

*Lieberman, E. James. **Guía sexual para jóvenes y del control de la natalidad.** Barcelona: Martínez Roca, 1979.
224p. $D.
Translation of **Sex and Birth Control, A Guide for the
Young.** Has good coverage of sex, birth control, and
venereal disease. Answers the most asked questions by
teenagers. Addresses one's responsibility to oneself and to
others, and the consequences of one's actions. There is
also some discussion of alternative lifestyles to monogamy.

Serrat, Luis. **Educación y vida sexual.** Barcelona: CEAC,
1976. 233p. (Nueva Enciclopedia Femenina). $D.
Detailed treatment of the emotional and physical aspects
of sex.

613.2—DIETETICS

Andrews, Allen. **Conserve y vigile su peso.** México: Olimpo,
    1977. 127p. $E.
Translation of **Slimming the Easy Way.** Common sense
advice on losing weight.

*Hauser, Benjamin Gayelord. **Método dietético.** Barcelona:
    Bruguera, 1979. 273p. $D.
Translation of **Look Younger, Live Longer.** Sound advice
for a healthier and happier mature age. One of the early
health bestsellers that is still popular in Spanish.

613.4—PERSONAL BEAUTY

*Meredith, Bronwen. **Vogue salud y belleza.** Barcelona: Fo-
    lio, 1981. 340p. HB. $A.
Translation of **Vogue Body and Beauty Book.** A quality
book on all aspects of body maintenance and beauty. Expensive but well worth the price.

*Salud y belleza.** Barcelona: Bruguera, 1980. 213p. (Libro
    práctico). $E.
The emphasis here is on health. Cautions against the
use of expensive commercial products that are potentially
hazardous. Recommends natural beauty aids and a healthful
program of exercise, good nutrition, and rest. Very readable; often humorous.

Stangl, Marie-Luise. **Descubre tu belleza.** León, España:
    Everest, 1983. 288p. $D.
A guide to cosmetics, hair care, exercise, hygiene, and
nutrition.

613.71—EXERCISE

Enciclopedia completa de ejercicios. Madrid: EDAF, 1980.
    335p. $B.
Translation of the Diagram Groups' **The Complete
Encyclopedia of Exercises.** Many exercises are illustrated
in black and white.

Mera Carrasco, Julio. **Gimnasia para la mujer.** México: Libro-Mex, 1980. 84p. (Manual práctico). $E.
Covers basic exercises for women, including those for "problem areas," and emphasizes health maintenance. Part of an inexpensive series of books on exercise that is also published by Mexicanos Unidos.

Sala Comas, José. **Adquiera músculos en 30 días.** Barcelona: Alas, 1980. 64p. $E.
Discusses the very popular topic of weightlifting.

*Sullivan, Kenneth. **Ejercicios para vivir mejor.** Barcelona: Martínez Roca, 1980. 208p. (Nueva Fontana). $E.
Includes specialized exercises for spot weight reduction, muscle toning, and individual sports, as well as general fitness programs for different age groups.

*Thomas, Vaughan. **Como mantenerse en forma.** Barcelona: Blume, 1981. 95p. (Pequeñas guías prácticas). $E.
Translation of **Book of Fitness and Exercise.** A well-illustrated guide to exercises for general fitness, with sections on specific needs such as flexibility, strength, and endurance. Recommended especially for the sports-minded.

613.79—RELAXATION

Hewitt, James. **Relajación: cómo la naturaleza hace frente a la tensión.** Madrid: EDAF, 1980. 125p. (Plus Vitae). $E.
An easy-to-read guide for relieving stress. Gives suggestions on physical and mental exercises, good nutrition, and ways to improve one's environment.

613.9—FAMILY PLANNING

Billings, Evelyn. **Método Billings; control natural de la fertilidad.** Buenos Aires: Emecé, 1982. 230p. $C.
Translation of **The Billings Method,** a Roman Catholic church approved method of natural birth control.

*Evitar el embarazo: ABC de la anticoncepción. Madrid: Altalena, 1980. 90p. (Maraflash). $D.
Comprehensive yet concise discussion of contraception. Methods are described in detail, and drawings and notes on effectiveness and side effects are included. The attitude of the Roman Catholic Church is also discussed.

615.11—PHARMACOPEIAS

Rosenstein, Emilio. **Diccionario de especialidades farmacéuticas.** México: P.L.M., 1983. 1408p. $A.
Similar to the **Physician's Desk Reference.** Gives detailed descriptions of different types of drugs and their use.

615.535—NATUROPATHY

Lazaeta Acharan, Manuel. **La medicina natural al alcance de todos.** México: Pax-México, 1978. 479p. $C.
A classic title on natural medicine. The author does not believe in antibiotics, X-rays, surgery, or herbal cures. He instead stresses maintaining health and helping the body cure itself with vapor baths, diet, air, sun, and water.

*Maury, Emmerick A. **Diccionario familiar de medicina natural.** Barcelona: Martínez Roca, 1981. 441p. (Fontana Práctica). $D.
The first part of the book describes therapies that involve acupuncture, homeopathy, vitamins, medicinal plants, climate, and baths. The second part describes common ailments and their prevention and cure through different therapies. There are warnings throughout the book to seek a doctor's advice. Excellent.

615.78—DRUGS AFFECTING THE NERVOUS SYSTEM

Ropp, Robert S. **Las drogas y la mente.** México: Continental, 1980. 299p. $B.

Discusses the use of drugs in religion, folklore, therapy, and escape, and explains their effect on the human mind.

615.822—MECHANOTHERAPY AND THERAPEUTIC MASSAGE

*Dalet, Roger. **Mejore su salud y su belleza con una simple presión de dedo.** Madrid: Daimón, 1980. 167p. $D.
Translated from the French. Deals mainly with the use of acupressure for beauty maintenance. Illustrates pressure points used for losing weight, for eliminating dry skin, wrinkles, acne, and freckles and for preventing varicose veins and baldness.

615.892—ACUPUNCTURE

Beau, Georges. **Acupuntura: la medicina China.** Barcelona: Martínez Roca, 1975. 191p. $E.
This fascinating discussion of the history and philosophy of acupuncture was originally published in France, where most of the Western world's research on this Chinese medical technique has been done.

616—DISEASES

*Bierge, José. **Medicina para todos: esperando al médico.** Barcelona: Sopena, 1979. 761p. (Biblioteca Hispania Ilustrada). HB. $C.
An excellent, intermediately priced guide to diseases. Describes ailments through the use of illustrations.

Clark, R.L. **El libro de la salud; una enciclopedia médica para todos.** México: Continental, 1981. 982p. HB. $A.
Translation of **The Book of Health.** This standard reference work for the layperson describes and prescribes treatment for almost all health problems and diseases.

Enciclopedia familiar de la medicina y la salud. New York: Stuttman, 1967. 2v. HB. $A.
Translation of the **Modern Family Health Guide,** which

contains articles on major health topics written by medical experts. While easy to use, it does not have information on medical breakthroughs during the last 15 years.

Gómez, Joan. **Diccionario de síntomas.** Barcelona: Acervo, 1980. 681p. HB. $A.
Translation of the **Dictionary of Symptoms.** Includes special sections on men, women, and children. Describes symptoms, causes, and treatment.

Krupp, Marcus A. **Diagnóstico clínico y tratamiento.** México: Manual Moderno, 1984. 1204p. $A.
This expensive diagnostic and treatment manual for doctors contains much useful information not found in books written for the general public.

El manual Merck de diagnóstico y terapéutica. Rahway, N.J.: Merck, 1978. 2298p. HB. $A.
Translation of **The Merck Manual of Diagnosis and Therapy.** Not as detailed as **Diagnóstico clínico y tratamiento,** but it is similar and easier to acquire. New edition available in January 1986.

Serrat, Luis. **Consejero médico.** Barcelona: CEAC, 1976. 253p. (Enciclopedia femenina). $D.
Gives a brief description of major diseases, including causes, symptoms, and treatment.

616.0252—First Aid

*American Medical Association. **Manual de primeros auxilios y cuidados de urgencia.** Madrid: EDAF, 1982. 281p. (Plus Vitae). $D.
The most complete first aid book in Spanish. Also useful because it refers to health facilities and centers in the United States.

Guía de primeros auxilios. Barcelona: Mundo Actual, 1980. 118p. HB. $C.
Translation of **Accident Action.** A well-illustrated first aid manual, with emphasis on safety and accident prevention.

616.1—Diseases of the Cardiovascular System

Enfermedades del corazón: su significado, causas y exitoso

tratamiento.   Madrid: EDAF, 1980.   113p.   (Plus Vitae).
$E.
Translation of **Heart Ailments**, prepared by Science of
Life Books, with emphasis on preventing heart disease.

Haid, Helmut.   **Enfermedades venosas.**   Barcelona: Mundo
Actual, 1981.   154p. $D.
Discusses causes, treatments, and tests for circulatory
problems such as varicose veins, swollen or ulcerated legs,
and phlebitis.

616.132—Hypertension

Fritel, Didier.   **La hipertensión arterial.**   Bilbao: Mensaje-
jero, 1982.   173p. $D.
Discusses high blood pressure--definitions, identification, and treatment.

616.2—Diseases of the Respiratory System

Las alergias: conocerlas y superarlas.   Madrid: Altalena,
1980.   92p.   (Maraflash). $D.
On identifying and curing allergies.

Arnold, Edouard.   **Las enfermedades pulmonares.**   Barcelona:
Acervo, 1980.   173p.   (Acervo divulgación: serie me-
dicina). $D.
A clear, popular discussion of lung diseases.

Nolte, Dietrich.   **Asma: tratamiento óptimo y precóz de
todos los síntomas, como evitar el asma crónica y sus
consecuencias.** Barcelona: Mundo Actual, 1980.   104p.
(Consulta Médica). $D.
Translation of **Asthma.**   On treating the symptoms of
asthma and avoiding its effects.

616.462—Diabetes Mellitus

*****Manual de diabetes Joslin.**   México: Continental, 1980.
339p. $C.
Translation of **Joslin Diabetes Manual.**   One of the most
complete books on diabetes for the layperson in Spanish.
Covers diet, related ailments, treatment, drugs, and their
administration.

616.53—Diseases of the Sebaceous Glands

Hoehn, Gustave H. **Cure su acné.** Madrid: EDAF, 1981. 170p.
  (Plus Vitae). $E.
Translation of **Acne Can Be Cured,** which emphasizes good
nutrition.   Also published by Diana under the title **El acné
es curable.**

616.72—Diseases of the Joints

*Scott, James Thomas. **¿Qué hay de cierto sobre la artritis?**
  Bogotá: Norma, 1981. 158p. $D.
Translation of **Arthritis and Rheumatism.**

616.857—Migraine

Bernardi, Francoise. **Cúrate tu mismo los dolores de cabe-
  za.** Bilbao: Mensajero, 1981. 199p. (Manuales del
  Bienestar). $D.
Offers common sense advice on curing headaches.

616.895—Manic-Depressive Psychosis

Sturgeon, Wina. **Depresión: cómo identificarla, cómo curar-
  la, como superarla.** Barcelona: Grijalbo, 1981. 297p.
  (Autoayuda y superación). $D.
Translation of **Depression.** Of the many books in Spanish
on the subject, this title, by a well-known consumer
advocate, is well-researched and offers good coverage.

616.95—Venereal Diseases

*Barlow, David. **¿Qué hay de cierto sobre las enfermedades
  venéreas?** Bogotá: Norma, 1980. 158p. $D.
Aimed primarily at the layperson, this book contains
useful information on the causes, symptoms, and treatment of
syphilis, gonorrhea, and other sexually transmitted diseases.

616.994—Cancers

*Scott, Ronald Bodley, Sir. **¿Qué hay de cierto sobre el
  cáncer?** Bogotá: Norma, 1981. 222p. $D.
Translation of **Cancer.** An up-to-date review of advances

in the diagnosis and treatment of cancer, its types, symptoms, nature, and causes.

618.2—OBSTETRICS

Duprey, Yves. **Embarazo y parto.** Barcelona: Parramón, 1981. (Guía práctica de la salud). $D.
Offers a highly visual presentation of pregnancy and childbirth.

Kitzinger, Sheila. **Embarazo y parto.** México: Interamericana, 1982. 346p.
Translation of **Pregnancy and Childbirth.** A readable, well-illustrated, comprehensive discussion of the psychological, social, and physical aspects of childbirth. Includes sections on single parenthood, twins, and health problems.

*Merkl, Hellmuth. **Parto sin miedo.** León, España: Everest, 1970. 189p. (Club Everest). $E.
An excellent guide to childbirth, covering nutrition, exercise, and natural childbirth methods.

Nilsson, Lennart. **Un niño va a nacer.** Barcelona: Ayma, 1977. 260p. HB. $D.
Translation of **A Child Is Born.** A photographic description of the development of the fetus.

618.92—PEDIATRICS

*Shiller, Jack G. **Guía de las enfermedades infantiles.** Barcelona: Martínez Roca, 1982. 251p. (Fontana Práctica).
Translation of **Childhood Illness.** Describes common childhood illnesses and their treatment.

620.003—ENGINEERING DICTIONARIES

Collazo, Javier L. **Diccionario enciclopédico de términos técnicos inglés-español, español-inglés.** New York: McGraw-Hill, 1980. 3v. HB.

Although expensive, this is the most comprehensive bilingual dictionary of technical terms.

Mosqueira Roldán, Salvador. **Diccionario inglés-español, español-inglés de ingeniería.** México: Patria, 1969. 835p. HB. $B.
Includes technical terms used in engineering, carpentry, plumbing, hydraulics, mining, construction, railroading, and sheet metal work.

621.56—REFRIGERATION

*Goliber, P.F. **Mantenimiento y reparación de refrigeradores.** México: Diana, 1980. $D.
Explains refrigerator repair for home use and for those learning a trade.

629.03—AUTOMOTIVE DICTIONARIES

Lima, Robert F. **Arco Motor Vehicle Dictionary/Diccionario Arco del Automotor.** New York: Arco, 1980. 362p. $C.
Bilingual automotive dictionary.

629.26—MOTOR LAND VEHICLES AND CYCLES—BODIES AND BODY WORK

Villeger, Yvon. **Reparación de carrocerías: técnica y práctica.** Barcelona: CEAC, 1980. 296p. (Biblioteca CEAC del automóvil). $D.
A manual on automobile body work for the seasoned mechanic as well as the novice.

629.287—MOTOR LAND VEHICLES AND CYCLES—MAINTENANCE AND REPAIR

Barber, Derk. **Pequeñas reparaciones y mantenimiento del automóvil.** Barcelona: CEAC, 1982. 160p. (Biblioteca CEAC del automóvil). $D.
Instructions for common do-it-yourself auto maintenance procedures.

*Chilton guía para la reparación y afinación.** México: Limusa, 1981. $D.
Translation of **Chilton's Repair and Tune-Up Guide** series. Guides for the following cars have been published in Spanish: Chevrolet 1968-1979, Datsun 1973-1980, Ford 1968-1979, Rabbit Scirocco 1975-1978, and Volkswagen 1970-1979.

Chilton manual de reparación de automóviles 1976-1983. México: Limusa, 1984. 1334p. $A.
Translation of **Chilton's Auto Repair Manual 1983.** Contains detailed information on the repair of American and foreign cars.

Crouse, William Harry. **El libro del automóvil.** Barcelona: Marcombo, 1980. 596p. $A.
Translation of **The Auto Book.** Although expensive, this is a high quality book on how an automobile is built, how it works, and how to repair it. Recommended for young mechanics and car owners.

*Nash, Frederick C. **Fundamentos de mecánica automotriz.** México: Diana, 1970. 308p. $D.
Translation of **Automotive Fundamentals.** Written for beginners in auto mechanics.

*Toboldt, William King. **Automótrix: manual de reparaciones automotrices.** Darien, Conn.: Lineal/Cleworth, 1983. 665p. HB. $A.
Offers information on automobile functions and construction, to facilitate diagnosis and repairs. Includes the major systems of the most popular models, as well as tune-up specifications.

Williams, John. **Pequeñas reparaciones y mantenimiento de la motocicleta.** Barcelona: CEAC, 1982. 232p. (Biblioteca CEAC del automóvil). $D.
Instructions for common motorcycle repairs.

632—PLANT INJURIES, DISEASES, PESTS

Philbrick, Helen. **El libro de los insectos.** México: CECSA,
1981. $D.
Translation of **The Bug Book,** published by Garden Way. A
general introduction to the insect world. Explains how to
identify insects and how to control pests.

635—GARDEN CROPS

Bonar, Ann. **Cómo cultivar las hortalizas.** Barcelona:
Blume, 1981. 95p. (Pequeñas guías prácticas). $E.
Translation of **Book of Vegetable Gardening.** Although
small, this book offers much good, basic information on soil
preparation and on the selection and care of vegetables.
Ample illustrations.

*Bonar, Ann. **Cómo practicar la jardinería.** Barcelona:
Blume, 1981. 95p. (Pequeñas guías prácticas). $E.
Translation of **Book of Basic Gardening.** Written by a
well-known British expert on gardening, this guide offers
basic information in a well-illustrated format.

Guía práctica ilustrada para el jardín. Barcelona: Blume,
1979. 2v. $A.
Although this is an excellent book on flower and
vegetable gardening, especially in regard to plant selection
and growing seasons, it applies mainly to the eastern half
of the United States.

Guillen Andreu, Roberto. **Plantas hortícolas.** Valencia:
Floraprint, 1980. 143p. HB. $C.
An attractive and useful book on vegetable gardening.
The hybrid varieties of vegetables mentioned are not found
in the United States, but otherwise the information is good.
This is part of an excellent series on gardening,
particularly applicable to California because of its
Mediterranean climate. Other titles in the Floraprint series
are: **Plantas de interior, Plantas mediterráneas, Plantas
vivaces, Rosales, Arboles de ornamento, Arbustos de
ornamento,** and **Coníferas ornamentales.**

Ritte, Louis. **Cultivo intensivo de huertos pequeños.**
México: CECSA, 1980. $D.

Translation of **Success with Small Food Gardens**. Explains techniques for intensive food gardening in small garden plots: plant selection, soil preparation, garden planning, edible decorative plants, and money saving tips.

635.933347—Cactuses

Ballester Olmos, José Francisco. **Los cactus y las otras plantas suculentas.** Valencia: Floraprint, 1978. 142p. HB. $C.
The information on each succulent includes a color photograph; a description of the flower, its habitat, and growing medium; optimal sunlight, watering, and temperature needs, and method of multiplication. Also has general information on care, including disease prevention.

635.965—Houseplants

*Baines, Jocelyn. **El ABC de las plantas de interior.** Madrid: Blume, 1980. 191p. $C.
Translation of **The ABC's of House and Conservatory Plants.** Describes indoor plants and their care. Each plant is pictured in vibrant color, and plants are arranged alphabetically by Latin name, which is preferred because of the variance in regional names throughout the Spanish-speaking world.

636—ANIMAL HUSBANDRY

Belanger, Jerome D. **Cría de ganado menor: usted también puede criar cabras, pollos, ovejas, conejos, guajolotes y otros animales domésticos.** México: Diana, 1978. 267p. $D.
Translation of **Small Livestock.** Covers the selection, breeding, housing, feeding, and health care of goats, chickens, sheep, rabbits, turkeys, ducks, geese, guinea hens, pigeons and pigs. Describes also the production and processing of meat, eggs, and milk. Excellent for small farms or backyards where livestock are allowed.

636.39—Goats

Belanger, Jerome D. **Cría moderna de cabras lecheras.** México: CECSA, 1981. 171p. $D.
Translation of **Raising Milk Goats the Modern Way.** Covers selection, nutrition, and care, as well as milk and meat production.

636.68—Cage and Aviary Birds

Santilli, Grazia. **Mis amigos los pájaros.** Madrid: Susaeta, 1975. 46p. (Colección Primavera). HB. $E.
Similar to **Mis amigos los gatos**, this title serves as an introduction to the care of birds. Has a brief section on tropical fish.

636.6862—Finches (Canaries)

Fritsch, Otto Von. **Canarios: adquisición, cuidados, enfermedades, nutrición y canto.** Madrid: Altalena, 1982. 68p. (Fauna doméstica). $D.
An attractive, easy-to-read book to aid in the selection, care, and understanding of canaries. Also explains how to get them to sing.

*Newby, Cliff. **Los canarios, cómo seleccionarlos y cuidarlos.** Barcelona: Hispano Europea, 1977. 112p. (Colección Herakles). $E.
Discusses the care and selection of canaries.

636.6865—Parrots

Roberti, Marina. **Cría moderna de periquitos, loros y papagayos.** Barcelona: De Vecchi, 1976. 135p. $D.
Discusses the care of parakeets and parrots.

636.7—Dogs

The American Kennel Club. **Enciclopedia canina, el gran libro del perro.** México: Diana, 1982. 637p. $A.
Dog breeds are fully described. Includes black and white photographs and qualifications for competition.

*Duncan, Lee. **Cuidado y educación del perro.** México: Continental, 1981. 244p. $C.
Translation of **The Rin Tin Tin Book of Dog Care.**

Although a bit too cute, it does offer good information on the selection, care, and training of the family dog.

*Jones, Arthur F. **Cuidado y educación de los perros.** México: Diana, 1977. 327p. $C.
Translation of **Care and Training of Dogs.** Expert advice on how to choose, feed, train, care for, and handle a dog.

Palmer, Joan. **La gran enciclopedia del perro.** Barcelona: Parramón, 1981. 242p. HB. $A.
A profusely illustrated book on dog breeds and their care. Excellent for browsing or for general information.

Wratten, Peggy. **Los perros.** Barcelona: Castell, 1980. 62p. (La naturaleza). $E.
An inexpensive but beautiful browsing item on dogs.

636.73—Working Dogs

El perro pastor alemán. Barcelona: Parramón, 1981. 128p. $D.
A well-illustrated book on the origin, characteristics, diseases, and training of the German Shepherd.

Spirer, Louis Ziegler. **Todo sobre el Dobermann Pinscher.** Barcelona: Hispano Europea, 1981. 344p. $D.
A complete book on the Dobermann Pinscher, including selection, breeding, training, characteristics, and diseases.

636.8—Cats

Santilli, Grazia. **Mis amigos los gatos.** Madrid: Susaeta, 1975. 47p. (Colección Primavera). HB. $E.
A brief but colorfully illustrated introduction to the breeds and care of cats. Also includes information on hamsters, white mice, turtles, and squirrels. Suitable for older children and adults who need **very** basic information.

Fritzche, Helga. **Gatos: compra, cuidados, alimentación y enfermedades.** Madrid: Altalena, 1982. 72p. $E.
Discusses the selection, care, and feeding of cats.

636.9322—Rabbits

Netherway, Marjorie E. **Cría casera de conejos.** Barcelona: Aura, 1978. 78p. (Inversiones caseras). $E.

Translation of **Home Rabbit Keeping**, for the backyard farmer. Describes the selection, care, feeding, housing, killing, and processing of rabbits.

639.344—FRESHWATER AQUARIUMS

Braemer, Helga. **Peces de acuario: acuarios de agua dulce, selección de peces y su cuidado.** Madrid: Altalena, 1982. 69p. (Fauna doméstica). $D.
An inexpensive, attractive, and informative guide for the selection and care of the freshwater aquarium.

640—HOME ECONOMICS AND FAMILY LIVING

*Seymour, John. **Guía práctica ilustrada para la vida en el campo.** Barcelona: Blume, 1979. 256p. $C.
Translation of **The Complete Book of Self Sufficiency.** Offers much more than just basic facts on gardening and agriculture. Has much useful information difficult to find in Spanish or found only in specialized sources. Some of the subjects covered are: care of farm animals, beekeeping, food conservation, production of natural energy, curing leather, and making fabrics, baskets, bricks, tiles, ponds, beer, wine, ovens, and cheese. Profusely illustrated.

641.1—APPLIED NUTRITION

Bender, Arnold E. **Guía de las calorías y de la nutrición.** Barcelona: Folio, 1981. 128p. (Guías de bolsillo Folio). HB. $D.
Translation of **The Pocket Guide to Calories and Nutrition.**

Diccionario de los alimentos. Barcelona: Cedel, 1979. 760p. $D.
One of the best books in Spanish on the nutritive value of foods. Includes the history, composition, conservation, benefits, and drawbacks of individual foods.

*Wade, Carlson. **Vitaminas y otros complementos alimentarios y su salud.** New Canaan, Conn.: Keats, 1980. 115p. $D. Translation of **Vitamins and Other Food Supplements.** Offers a table of foods and their composition, in a pocket size edition.

641.59—INTERNATIONAL COOKERY

*Cocina Hispanoamericana/American-Spanish Cookbook.** Barcelona: Garriga, 1967. 339p. HB. $A.
Rather expensive, but this is one of the few Spanish cookbooks that has recipes for American food.

Gandulfo, Petrona C. de. **El libro de Doña Petrona: recetas de arte culinario.** Buenos Aires: s.n., 1982. 821p. $A.
This title, considered the classic cookbook of Argentina, is in its 75th printing.

Gook, Roland. **Las cien recetas de cocina más famosas del mundo.** León, España: Everest, 1980. 109p. HB. $C.
A beautifully illustrated book presenting the 100 most famous recipes in the world.

Kruger, Arne. **El placer de cocinar.** Barcelona, Mundo Actual, 1980. 249p. HB. $A.
One of the most beautiful cookbooks in Spanish. Expensive but well worth the price, as each dish is pictured in vibrant color. Besides containing many international recipes, there are sections on company dishes, party foods, everyday menus, diet dishes, bar drinks, table, setting and basic cooking techniques.

Pinkham, Mary Ellen. **Mil y un consejo prácticos en la cocina.** México: Lasser, 1981. Spiralbound. $D.
Translation of **Mary Ellen's Best of Helpful Kitchen Hints.** Contains useful recipes, and ideas for removing spots, saving burned and salty foods, and solving kitchen problems.

Ramos Espinosa, Virginia. **Recetas para la buena mesa.** México: Diana, 1979. 495p. $D.
Written by a Mexican cooking authority. Contains mostly Mexican recipes, but also includes many international dishes that have a Mexican flavor.

641.5951—Cookery of China

Lo, Kenneth. **Cocina china rápida y fácil.** Barcelona: Martínez Roca, 1982. 189p. (Fontana práctica). $D.
Includes sample menus, recipes, equipment, and techniques of Chinese cooking.

641.5972—Cookery of Mexico

Molinar, Rita. **Dulces mexicanos.** México: Pax-Mexico, 1969.
  365p. $E.
Contains recipes for all types of candies and desserts from all regions of Mexico. The prologue describes the origin of the Mexican sugar industry and of some of the sweets. Includes puddings, fruits, beverages, pies, cakes, preserves, and juices. Indexed by type of sweet and by region.

*Romo de Escamilla, Adela. **La cocina de Doña Adela: recetario de la cocinera práctica.** México: CECSA, 1979.
  309p. $C.
A classic cookbook from Mexico. Although the emphasis is on Mexican cooking, international recipes are included.

*Rosa, Angeles de la. **Especialidades de la cocina mexicana.**
  México: Mexicanos Unidos, 1976. 215p. $E.
Editores Mexicanos Unidos publishes several cookbooks on the regional cooking of Mexico. This one includes all types of dishes and beverages. Indexed by region and by type of dish.

641.597291—Cookery of Cuba

Cocina al minuto. Miami: Cubaamérica, n.d. 319p. $D.
International recipes with a Cuban flavor. Many call for prepared mixes and canned food.

641.597291—Cookery of Puerto Rico

Cabanillas, Berta. **Cocine a gusto.** 14. ed. Río Piedras, P.R.: Universitaria, 1980. 326p. HB. $C.
A compilation of traditional Puerto Rican recipes.

641.5980—Cookery of Latin America

Fonseca, Nuri. **Recetas de América Latina.** México: Concepto, 1978. 229p. $D.
These Latin American specialties are arranged under
appetizers, soups, sauces, eggs, salads, vegetables, sea-
food, meats, and desserts.

641.815—BREADS

*Brown, Edward. **El libro del pan tassajara.** Madrid: EDAF,
1982. $D.
Translation of **The Tassajara Bread Book.** Explains basic
breadmaking techniques and includes recipes for all types of
whole-grain breads, muffins, popovers, crackers, and bagels.

641.83—SALADS

Klever, Ulrich. **El gran libro de las ensaladas: todo sobre
el arte de preparar ensaladas, las mejores ideas del
mundo 1001 variaciones.** Barcelona: Mundo Actual, 1981.
161p. HB. $C.
A nicely illustrated guide to making all types of
salads, such as fruit, vegetable, meat, and pasta. Covers
the selection of ingredients, method of preparation, and
presentation.

641.8653—CAKES

Alvarado, Marithé de. **Arte mexicano del azúcar.** México:
CECSA, 1982. 728p. $A.
Advanced cake decorating by an authority in the field.

Wilton Enterprises. **Decoración de bizcochos: una guía para
principiantes.** Woodbridge, Ill.: n.s., 1982. 35p. $E.
A beginner's guide to cake decorating.

642.6—TABLE SERVICE

Aiken, Brenton R. **Manual del mesero y la mesera.** México: Diana, 1980. 156p. $D.
Translation of **The Waiter/Waitress Manual.** Contains much information that a food service employee should know, such as setting tables, taking food orders, interpreting menus, using math, and maintaining hygiene. Includes different types of restaurants, from four-star establishments to fast food chains.

643.16—HOME SECURITY

Family Handyman Magazine. **Seguridad total en el hogar.** Madrid: Mapfre, 1982. 241p. $B.
Translation of **Total Home Security.** Excellent advice for the do-it-yourselfer on home and automobile protection from burglary and fire.

643.6—APPLIANCES AND LABOR SAVING INSTALLATIONS

Pey i Estrani, Santiago. **Electricidad y electrodomésticos.** Barcelona: CEAC, 1980. 176p. (Enciclopedia del bricolaje). $D.
On the maintenance and repair of common household appliances.

Wheeler, Gershon J. **Reparación de electrodomésticos.** Barcelona: Marcombo, 1981. 202p. $C.
Translation of **How to Repair Electrical Appliances.** Explains the fundamentals of electricity, and provides instructions for repairing appliances, such as electric blankets, waffle irons, coffeemakers, toasters, blenders, electric knives, and clothes dryers. Uses a do-it-yourself approach.

643.7—Appliances and Labor Saving Installations—Maintenance and Repair

Dominique, Colette. **Mientras llega el fontanero.** Barce-

lona: Caralt, 1981. 233p. (Biblioteca práctica
Caralt). HB. $D.
Similar to **Recipes for Home Repair**, sections are divided
by type of repair, such as carpentry, roofing, painting, and
fixing small appliances.

*Jackson, Albert. **Guía práctica ilustrada para el mantenimiento y conservación de la casa.** Barcelona: Blume,
1981. 256p. $C.
Translation of **Good Housekeeping Do-it-Yourself Book.**
An extremely well-illustrated book on interior decoration
and repair and maintenance around the home.

Pey i Estrani, Santiago. **Fontanería y albañilería.** Barcelona: CEAC, 1977. 207p. (Enciclopedia del bricolaje). $D.
Describes plumbing and masonry for the home repairman.

645—FURNISHING AND DECORATING THE HOME

Pey i Estrani, Santiago. **Revestimiento de suelos, paredes y
techos.** Barcelona: CEAC, 1982. 142p. (Enciclopedia
del bricolaje). $D.
All types of wall and floor coverings and their
application are shown in many black-and-white illustrations.

645.1—Floor Coverings

Galy, Michel. **Todo para arreglar los suelos.** Bilbao:
Mensajero, 1981. 189p. (Colección Hágalo Ud. mismo).
$D.
Illustrates techniques for installing floor coverings,
such as carpeting, parqueting, cork, tile, and linoleum.

645.2—Coverings for Walls and Ceilings

Galy, Michel. **Todo para vestir las paredes.** Bilbao:
Mensajero, 1981. 189p. (Colección Hágalo Ud. mismo).
$D.
Contains fairly good instructions for painting,
wallpapering, and installing tile, mirrors, and paneling.

Pey i Estrani, Santiago. **Pintura y empapelado.** Barcelona:
CEAC, 1982. 202p. (Enciclopedia del bricolaje). $D.

Painting and wallpapering for the homeowner are demonstrated in many black-and-white illustrations.

645.4—Furniture and Accessories

Howes, C. **Práctica del tapizado.** Barcelona: CEAC, 1980. 165p. $D.
Translation of **Practical Upholstery.** Illustrates many different upholstery techniques, materials, and equipment. Excellent for home use.

Pey i Estrani, Santiago. **Ebanistería y tapizado.** Barcelona: CEAC, 1982. 176p. (Enciclopedia del bricolaje). $D.
Explains do-it-yourself cabinet making and upholstering.

646.4—CLOTHING CONSTRUCTION

*Lynch, Mary. **Costura simplificada: método sencillo de costura.** México: General, 1970. 213p. $D.
Translation of **Sewing Made Easy.** Covers selecting a pattern and making alterations. Discusses necessary equipment, differences in materials, basics for sewing by hand and machine, and other sewing techniques.

Tararilla Rey, J. **Vestir es fácil.** Barcelona: CEAC, 1981. 225p. (Colección Libros Femeninos). $D.
Contains money-saving suggestions for making dresses and gowns with very little sewing. The dresses are modelled by ordinary people. Especially useful in preparing for graduations, proms, and quinceañeras.

646.724—CARE OF HAIR

Milady Publishing Corporation. **Técnicas modernas del peinado.** New York: Milady, 1977. 474p. $B.
Describes hair care and cutting techniques for beauticians.

646.726—COSMETOLOGY

Colletti, Anthony B. **La cosmetología: la guía Keystone para aprender el arte de embellecer.** New York: Keystone, 1979. 392p. HB. $C.
Translation of **Cosmetology, the Keystone Guide to Beauty Culture,** a textbook for those learning to become beauticians.

Milady Publishing Corporation. **Cosmetologists' State Board Exam Review/Repaso de la junta estatal de cosmetólogos.** New York: Milady, 1981. 128p. $C.
Bilingual study guide for the state board exam for cosmetologists.

649.1—HOME CARE OF CHILDREN

Leach, Penelope. **El bebé y el niño.** Barcelona: Argos Vergara, 1980. 557p. (Enciclopedia médica familiar). HB. $A.
Translation of **Baby and Child.** An excellent guide to child development. Offers a sympathetic look at children, and encourages parents to see their child's point of view and use common sense.

Leonard, Margaret. **Los primeros días del bebé.** México: Universo, 1980. 140p. $E.
Translation of **Your Baby's Early Days.** Describes basic child care routines and feeding.

Mi hijo de 3 a 6 años. Madrid: Altalena, 1980. 89p. $D.
A concise, easy-to-read examination of the physical, social, and emotional development of the child from three to six years of age.

Mi hijo de uno a tres años. Madrid: Altalena, 1980. 89p. $D.
Similar to the previous title, but for the child aged one to three years.

Novoa Bodet, José. **Mi hijo no quiere comer.** México: Diana, 1978. 140p. $E.
Provides helpful information for parents having problems getting their child to eat. Does not cover adolescent problems such as anorexia nervosa.

*Novoa Bodet, José. **¿Qué debe comer mi hijo?** México: Diana, 1981. 141p. $E.
An easy-to-read guide for parents on nutrition for children from birth to adolescence.

Payne, Alma. **El secreto de la alimentación infantil.** México: Posada, 1984. 173p. $D.
Translation of the **Baby Food Book.** Recipes and instructions for making baby food at home. Mostly for Mexican readers.

*Pensando en su niño.** Panamá: América, 1982. 448p. $E.
Contains a wealth of information on child care: diseases, infant care, personality development, discipline, preparation for school, etc. The least expensive of the general child care books, but it has no index.

*Silver-Kempe, Henry. **El primer año de nuestro hijo.** León, España: Everest, 1978. 177p. (Club Everest). $D.
Discusses baby care and development during the first year of life. Chapters on each month of a baby's life offer clear, concise explanations. Especially good for new parents.

Smith, Landon. **Alimente a sus hijos correctamente.** México: Edivisión, 1981. 299p. $C.
Translation of **Feed Your Kids Right.** Details the importance of certain nutrients in maintaining health, and explains how ailments can be treated with vitamins.

*Spock, Benjamin. **Tu hijo.** Madrid: Daimón, 1980. 502p. $D.
Translation of **The Common Sense Book of Baby and Child Care.** Although not an authoritative work on disciplining children, this classic offers a generous amount of information on the physical aspects of child rearing. Indispensable in any Spanish collection.

649.151—Home Care of Children With Physical Handicaps

Spock, Benjamin. **El cuidado del niño lisiado.** México: Prensa Médica, 1967. 206p. $E.
Translation of **Caring for Your Disabled Child.** A guide to understanding and helping the disabled child in his or her education, social adjustment, and rehabilitation.

649.5—Activities and Recreation

Arce, Carlos de. **Juegue con sus hijos.** Barcelona: Martínez Roca, 1982. 219p. $D.
Contains games, activities, and crafts to do with children.

Funes, Diego. **Como jugar y divertirse con los niños en un largo viaje en coche.** Madrid: Altalena, 1980. 90p. (Divertimento). $D.
Describes old and new games to play with children on a long car trip. The emphasis is on tongue twisters, riddles, guessing games, and word plays.

650.1—PERSONAL SUCCESS IN BUSINESS

*Mandlawitz, Lynda K. **Como conseguir el empleo que usted desea.** New York: R. Rosen, 1980. 124p. HB. $D.
Translation of **How to Find the Job You Want.** Information on searching the classified ads, writing a resumé, filling out a job application, interviewing, and locating job opportunities.

651—OFFICE SERVICES

*Prácticas de oficina: versión abreviada del libro "Técnicas secretariales y procedimientos de oficina". Cincinnati: Southwestern, 1982. 247p. HB. $C.
Based on **Secretarial Office Procedures.** Describes secretarial techniques and office procedures, including applying for a secretarial job and using office machines.

651.374—Secretarial and Related Services

*Doris, Lillian. **Manual completo de la secretaria.** México: CECSA, 1973. 583p. $A.
Translation of **The Complete Secretary's Handbook.** Covers correspondence; office etiquette; filing; record keeping; typing tips, U.S. shipping and mailing information; telephone, telegraph, and cable usage; report and legal form preparation; writing style; travel arranging; grammar; forms of address; and much more.

651.53—Filing Systems and Procedures

Q. de Gorbea, Josefina. **Sistemas de archivar y control de documentos.** Cincinnati: Southwestern, 1977. 227p. HB. $C.
Based on **Business Filing and Record Control.**

651.75—Correspondence

*Steel de Meza, Bárbara. **Business Letter Handbook Spanish-English/Manual de correspondencia comercial español-inglés.** New York: Regents, 1973. 195p. $D.
A very useful book for both Spanish- and English-speaking business people. Includes advice on letter writing and many sample letters for different occasions and needs.

652.3—TYPEWRITING

*Santiago Pérez, Aída. **Mecanografía siglo 21, curso básico.** Cincinnati: Southwestern, 1979. 42p. HB. $C.
Based on the Century 21 first year typing course. **Curso elemental e intermedio** (beginning and intermediate course), published in 1982, is also available.

653.427—SHORTHAND

Gregg, John Robert. **Taquigrafía Gregg, primer curso.** México: McGraw-Hill, 1969. 367p. $C.
Gregg's shorthand course. **Segundo curso** (second course), published in 1970, is also available.

657—ACCOUNTING

Contabilidad práctica del siglo XX, curso elemental. Cincinnati: Southwestern, 1974. 492p. HB. $B.
Translation of **20th Century Bookkeeping and Accounting.** A basic textbook on accounting methods. **Curso avanzado** (advanced course) is also available.

Fields, Louis. **Contabilidad simplificada.** México: CECSA, 1969. 181p. $E.
Translation of **Bookkeeping Made Simple.** A popular bookkeeping guide especially recommended for small businesses.

657.03—Accounting Dictionaries

Blanes Prieto, Joaquín. **Diccionario de términos contables, inglés–español y español–inglés/Dictionary of Accounting Terms, English–Spanish and Spanish–English.** México: CECSA, 1972. 393p. $C.
A bilingual dictionary of accounting terms.

658.3—PERSONNEL MANAGEMENT

Bolles, Richard Nelson. ¿De qué color es tu paracaidas? México: Diana, 1983. 230p. $D.
Translation of **What Color Is Your Parachute?** An extremely useful guide for people seeking employment, or a career change. Covers procedures for job hunting and self analysis of skills and temperament to guide individuals in their job selection.

Ecker, H. Paul. **Manual para supervisores.** México: Diana, 1971. 1982 reprint. $E.
Good advice for supervisors at all levels on such topics as motivation, training, communication, and solving difficulties with employees. Translation of **Handbook for Supervisors.**

660.021—TABULATED AND RELATED TECHNOLOGIES

Recetario industrial: enciclopedia. Refundición española de las obras "Henley's Twentieth Century Formulas, Recipes and Processes y "The Scientific American Cyclopedia of Formulas". Barcelona: Gili, 1979. 1335p. HB. $A.
Contains several thousand household, workshop, and scientific formulas, trade secrets, chemical recipes, and processes.

74   Technology (Applied Sciences)

671.52—WELDING

Griffin, Ivan H. **Técnicas para soldar tubería.** México:
    Diana, 1981. 113p. $D.
Translation of **Pipe Welding Techniques.** A general
introduction to different welding techniques.

Guiachino, Joseph. **Técnica y práctica de la soldadura.** Bar-
    celona: Reverté, 1981. 463p. $A.
Translation of **Welding Skills and Practices,** an
excellent textbook for those learning to be welders.

Love, L. Carl. **Soldadura procedimientos y aplicaciones.**
    México: Diana, 1981. 220p. $D.
Translation of **Welding, Procedures and Applications.**
Keeps technical theory at a minimum and explains basic
procedures.

674.43—PRODUCTION OF FINISHED LUMBER

Stokes, Gordon. **Práctica del torneado de la madera.** Bar-
    celona: CEAC, 1982. 139p. $D.
Translation of **Modern Wood Turning.** Provides step-
by-step instructions on woodturning for the amateur.

683.3—LOCKSMITHING

Ayuso, Carlos. **Cerrajería y herrajes en la construcción.**
    Barcelona: CEAC, 1981 225p. (Biblioteca de cons-
    trucción). $C.
A guide to installing locks and hinges on doors and
windows.

684.1—FURNITURE

Fabbro, Mario dal. **Como construir muebles por elementos:
    convertibles, acoplables, abatibles.** Barcelona: CEAC,
    1980. 262p. $D.
Translation of **How to Make Built-in Furniture.** Contains

plans and directions for the construction of 102 different types of built-in furniture.

Hayward, Charles Harold. **Carpintería y ebanistería prácticas.** Barcelona: CEAC, 1980. 192p. $D.
Describes the tools and the basics of carpentry and cabinet making.

Hayward, Charles Harold. **Restauración de muebles.** Barcelona: CEAC, n.d. 128p. $D.
A well-illustrated guide to restoring furniture.

693.1—MASONRY

Pey i Estrani, Santiago. **Albañilería.** Barcelona: CEAC, 1984. 178p. (Enciclopedia del bricolage). $C.
A guide to installing tile, bricks, and insulation.

700 Arts and Sports

708.972—GALLERIES, MUSEUMS OF MEXICO

Bernal, Ignacio. **Tesoros del Museo Nacional de Antropo-
logía de México.** Madrid: Daimón, 1971. 246p. HB. $A.
An excellent introduction to the art of Mexico. Describes the treasures of the Museum of Anthropology.

709—ART HISTORY

*Angel, Albalucía. **Visión del arte.** Barcelona: Jaimes
Libros, 1981. 127p. (Vidorama). HB. $C.
A good, brief introduction to art. Provides insight
into the great schools of art throughout history. Contains
many color illustrations on glossy paper. Older readers
will like the large print.

Azcárate Ristori, José María de. **Historia del arte.**
Madrid: Anaya, 1982. 1023p. HB. $A.
An excellent textbook discussion of the history of art.
Contains many black-and-white and color illustrations.

*Fernández, Justino. **El arte mexicano.** Middlesex, England:
Hamlyn House, 1968. 125p.
The great Mexican historian and art critic has put to-

gether an outstanding example of Mexico's artistic heritage, including ceramics, pyramids, sculptures, palaces, convents, churches, colonial paintings, and modern murals. Includes 59 excellent color photographs.

738.1—CERAMICS—TECHNIQUES, PROCEDURES, APPARATUS, EQUIPMENT, MATERIALS

Howell, Frank. **La artesanía de la cerámica: un enfoque de resolución de problemas de los aspectos fundamentales de la cerámica.** México: Continental, 1979. 173p. $C.
Translation of **The Craft of Pottery.** Describes pottery techniques by using a problem solving approach. Black-and-white photographs show procedures step by step.

Woody, Elsbeth S. **Cerámica a mano.** Barcelona: CEAC, 1981. 225p. (Enciclopedia de las artesanías). $D.
Translation of **Handbuilding Ceramic Forms.** Basic techniques of hand modeling are shown in black-and-white photographs.

738.917—Mexican Ceramics

Espejel, Carlos. **Cerámica popular mexicana.** Barcelona: Blume, 1975. 224p. (Colección nueva imágen). $A.
Beautifully illustrated coffee-table type of book on Mexican ceramics.

López Cervantes, González. **Cerámica mexicana.** México: Everest, 1983. 157p. $D.
Provides a beautiful overview of Mexican pottery from the pre-Hispanic days to the present folk art.

740—DRAWING

Llobera, José. **Dibujar es fácil.** Barcelona: AFHA, 1980. 3v. HB. $A.
Excellent set of books on all aspects of drawing.

Tubau Comalala, Iván. **Cómo utilizar los instrumentos de dibujo.** Barcelona: CEAC, 1978. 79p. (Pintando y dibujando). $D.

A large-format book on the uses of basic art implements, such as pencils, brushes, and paper. Other titles in this series are: **Dibujando animales** (drawing animals), **Dibujando niños** (drawing children), **Dibujando carteles** (drawing posters).

741.5—Cartoons, Caricatures, Comics

Jiménez, A. **Nueva picardía mexicana.** México: Mexicanos: Unidos, 1977. 302p. $E.
This title, along with **Picardía mexicana**, is the most read book of Mexican humor. It is a classic and is considered an important part of Mexican folklore.

Jiménez, A. **Picardía mexicana.** México: Mexicanos Unidos, 1978. 268p. $E.
The most popular title of Mexican humor. Now in its 69th printing.

Quino. **10 años con Mafalda.** México: Nueva Imágen, 1978. 190p. HB. $D.
Mafalda is rather like a sophisticated Dennis the Menace, a precocious child who is the bane of everyone around her. To Latin Americans, this comic strip character has the impact of Charlie Brown in the U.S. Also available as a 12 volume set.

Quino. **Gente en su sitio.** México: Nueva Imágen, 1981. $D.
The author is a famous humorist and caricaturist from Argentina. This particular title is reminiscent of Feiffer.

Rius. **Pequeño Rius ilustrado.** México: Grijalbo, 1979. 135p. $E.
Rius is the pseudonym of Eduardo del Río, a prolific Mexican satirist and caricaturist. Books like **Mao en su tinta** and **Cuba libre** evidence his socialist orientation. He is humorous, informal, and always appealing to the masses, which is a plus when he deals with serious subjects such as nutrition (**La panza es primero**) and ecology (**Cómo suicidarse sin maestro**).

745.0972—FOLK ART OF MEXICO

Martínez Peñaloza, Porfirio. **Arte popular de México: la**

creatividad artística del pueblo mexicano a través de los tiempos. México: Panorama, 1981. 154p. (Colección Panorama). $D.
Briefly traces the development of Mexican popular arts, and describes the techniques developed from Indian and Spanish cultures. Recommended, inexpensive title.

745.5—HANDICRAFTS

Enciclopedia de los trabajos manuales. Madrid: Reader's Digest, 1981. 423p. HB. $A.
Translation of **Reader's Digest Manual of Handicrafts.** Contains very basic descriptions of many crafts not found in other books in Spanish.

Faure, Valérie. **Cómo hacer objetos para regalo.** Barcelona: CEAC, 1978. 48p. (Manualidades). $E.
Contains instructions and ideas for making gifts. There are 28 titles in this series and some are suitable for use with children.

745.53—Handicrafts in Leather

Hamilton-Head, Ian. **Trabajo del cuero.** Barcelona: CEAC, 1981. 131p. (Enciclopedia CEAC de las artesanías). $D.
Translation of **Leatherwork.** A well-illustrated guide to the techniques and equipment used in working with leather.

745.542—Papier Maché

Kenny, Carla. **Arte del papel maché.** Barcelona: CEAC, 1978. 146p. (Enciclopedia CEAC de las artesanías). $D.
Translation of **The Art of Papier Maché.** One of the best books on papier maché in any language.

745.5933—Candles

Carey, Mary. **Cómo hacer velas.** Barcelona: Elfos, 1980. 64p. (Manualidades). $D.
Translation of **Candlemaking.** A well-illustrated guide to making all types of decorative candles. Other titles in

this series are: **Trabajos con cartón y papel** (crafts with cardboard and paper), **Cestería** (basketmaking), **Cómo hacer tus propios juegos** (how to make your own toys).

745.92—FLORAL ARTS

Vagg, Daphne. **Los arreglos florales.** Barcelona: Fontalba, 1980. 125p. (Guías Fontalba). HB. $D.
A fairly well-illustrated guide to flower arranging.

746—TEXTILE ARTS AND HANDICRAFTS

El arte de la aguja. Barcelona: Jaimes Libros, 1982. 124p. (Vidorama). HB. $C.
While this title is less detailed than **Guía práctica ilustrada para labores de hilo y aguja**, it is also less expensive and contains much basic information on sewing, embroidery, crocheting, petit point, and knitting.

*Brittain, Judy. **Guía práctica ilustrada para labores de hilo y aguja.** Barcelona: Blume, 1980. 2v. $A.
Translation of **Good Housekeeping Step-by-Step Encyclopedia of Needlework.** Volume one contains instructions for crocheting, tatting, macramé, knitting, braiding, netting, hooking rugs, and using a loom. Volume two describes embroidery, tapestry making, quilting, and basic sewing of dresses, draperies, tablecloths, and pillows. Purchased separately, each volume of this profusely illustrated set is moderately priced.

746.412—Basketry

Hart, Carol. **Cestería natural.** Barcelona: CEAC, 1981. 164p. (Enciclopedia CEAC de las artesanías). $D.
Instructions on making traditional as well as modern baskets from a variety of materials.

746.4222—Macramé

Gili, Mariona. **Arte y técnica del macramé.** Barcelona:

CEAC, 1982. 150p. (Enciclopedia CEAC de las artesanías). $D.
A well-illustrated, basic guide to the technique and materials used in macrame.

746.43—Knitting, Crocheting, Tatting

Short, Jacqueline. **Tejido creativo.** Barcelona: CEAC, 1981. 128p. (Enciclopedia CEAC de las artesanías). $D.
Translation of **Imaginative Weaving.** Shows how to make a design and work with paper, synthetic fibers, and other materials to make wall hangings and other decorative projects.

747—INTERIOR DECORATION

*King, Harold. **Cómo decorar el hogar.** Barcelona: Blume, 1981. 95p. (Pequeñas guías prácticas). $E.
Translation of **Book of Home Decorating.** A well-illustrated, basic book on painting, wallpapering, installing floors, and using color.

750.28—PAINTING

Hayes, Colin. **Guía completa de pintura y dibujo: técnicas y materiales.** Madrid: Blume 1981. 223p. $C.
Translation of **The Complete Guide to Painting and Drawing.** A very attractive book that will appeal to beginning art students.

Oltra Costa, Román. **Pintar es fácil.** Barcelona: AFHA, 1980. 2v. HB. $A.
Provides easy-to-follow instructions on how to paint.

751.45—OIL PAINTING

Tubau Comalala, Iván. **Los colores y los materiales en la pintura al óleo.** Barcelona: CEAC, 1978. 112p. (Enciclopedia de pintura al óleo). HB. $C.

Large format book on learning oil painting.   There are also other titles in this series.

760—GRAPHIC ARTS

Parramón, José María. **Así se dibujan letras, rótulos, logo-tipos.** Barcelona: Parramón 1980. 144p. (Colección aprender haciendo, Grafismo). $D.
A basic guide to drawing letters and making signs. Other titles in this series are: **Cómo dibujar la figura humana** (how to draw the human body) and **Cómo dibujar la cabeza humana** (how to draw the human head).

770—PHOTOGRAPHY

Hedgecoe, John. **Guía práctica de la fotografía.** Barcelona: Folio, 1981. 144p. (Guías de bolsillo Folio). HB. $D.
A handy guide to taking and developing photographs. For users of single lens reflex cameras.

El placer de fotografiar. Eastman Kodak Company, eds. Barcelona: Folio, 1980. 301p. $A.
Translation of **The Joy of Photography.** Contains a detailed description of camera equipment, picture taking techniques and film developing for 35mm single reflex cameras. Offers the most complete and best coverage of this subject available in one volume in Spanish.

780.1—PHILOSOPHY AND AESTHETICS OF MUSIC

Téllez Videras, José Luis. **Para acercarse a la música.** Barcelona: Salvat, 1981. 64p. (Temas clave). HB. $E.
Provides an understanding of music, its relationship to other forms of art. Covers the principles of music such as rhythm, harmony, counterpoint, melody and outlines the development of music forms such as the sonata, concerto and symphony. A well-illustrated and readable format.

780.9—HISTORICAL AND GEOGRAPHICAL TREATMENT OF MUSIC

*Cande, Roland de. **Invitación a la música: pequeño manual de iniciación.** Madrid: Aguilar, 1981. 307p. $C.
An excellent introductory survey of the history of music.

Nieves Falcón, Luis. **Mi música.** Illustrated by Rafael Rivera Rosa. San Juan, P.R.: Edil, 1975. 25p.
Describes the musical instruments, dances, songs, and music of Puerto Rico.

Reuter, Jas. **La música popular de México: origen e historia de la música que canta y toca el pueblo mexicano.** México: Panorama, 1980. 195p. (Colección Panorama). $D.
A brief overview of the history of the popular music of Mexico.

784.5—POPULAR SONGS

Jiménez, Armando. **Cancionero mexicano.** México: Libro-Mex, 1982. 4v. $C.
Contains an excellent selection of lyrics from old and new Mexican songs.

Ribes, Francisco, ed. **Canciones de España y América.** Illustrated by Perellon. Madrid: Santillana, 1965. 84p.
A carefully selected collection of 56 popular Spanish and Latin American songs and games for young readers. Splendid illustrations.

784.71972—FOLK SONGS OF MEXICO

Mendoza, Vicente T. **El corrido mexicano.** México: Fondo de Cultura Económica, 1954. 1974 reprint. 467p. $D.
The **corrido** is similar to the epic poems sung by the troubadours in the Middle Ages. Most **corridos** were created during the Mexican revolution when singers served as "newspapers" bringing tales of battles and heroic feats. Of interest to teachers and those looking for words of once familiar songs.

Mendoza, Vicente T. **Lírica infantil de México.** México:
Fondo de Cultura Económica, 1980. 214p. $D.
A collection of Mexican songs and nursery rhymes Mexico
compiled by a famous folklorist. Many include the music.

786.3—TRAINING IN AND PERFORMANCE ON KEYBOARD STRING INSTRUMENTS

*Evans, Roger. **Cómo tocar el piano: un modo nuevo y de fá-
cil comprensión para aprender a tocar el piano.** Madrid:
EDAF, 1982. 108p. $D.
A basic guide to learning to play the piano.

786.7—TRAINING IN AND PERFORMANCE ON ORGAN

Muñoz Bolanos, Jorge. **Qué fácil es aprender el órgano.** México: Servicios Editoriales Mexicanos, 1981. 135p. $D.
Provides instruction, through exercises and popular
songs, on how to play the organ. Chords and rhythms are included in appendixes.

786.97—ACCORDION AND CONCERTINA AND THEIR MUSIC

Estebarán, Antonio. **Método completo para acordeón.** Madrid: publ. by author, 1979. 88p. $C.
Contains exercises of increasing difficulty for learning
to play the 120-key (standard) accordion.

787.61—GUITAR

*Passos, Raúl. **Aprenda guitarra con canciones latinoame-
ricanas.** México: Mexicanos Unidos, 1979. 142p. $E.
An excellent book on learning to play the guitar. Not
only are all chords well illustrated, but there is also a
good selection of Latin American songs for practicing
different styles of playing.

791.53—PUPPETS

Casella, Norma. **Obras para teatro de títeres.** Buenos
Aires: Librería de Colegio, 1976. 108p. $D.
Contains scripts for puppet shows. Illustrated.

Philpott, Violet. **Cómo hacer y manejar marionetas.** Madrid:
PLESA, 1977. $E.
A well-illustrated, high-interest format book on making
puppets. Especially recommended for younger readers.

791.82—BULLFIGHTING

Díaz-Cañabate, Antonio. **El mundo de los toros.** León,
España: Everest, 1972. 195p. HB. $C.
A basic guide to bullfighting.

793.2—PARTIES AND ENTERTAINMENT

Kuhnemann, Ursula. **Un cumpleaños infantil.** Buenos Aires:
Kapelusz, 1975. 76p. (Colección cómo hacer). $E.
Contains helpful advice on all aspects of giving a
children's party, such as sending invitations, planning
theme parties, serving refreshments and providing enter-
tainment.

793.8—MAGIC

Scarne, John. **Trucos mágicos.** México: Diana, 1980. 329p.
$D.
Translation of **Scarne's Magic Tricks.** Contains
illustrated instructions on 200 magic tricks that involve
simple equipment.

794.1—CHESS

*Capablanca, José. **Fundamentos de ajedrez.** Madrid:
Aguilera, 1979. 206p. $D.
First published in 1921, this remains one of the best
books on chess, explaining general principles for beginners
as well as benefiting the experts.

795.4—CARD GAMES

Prat, Jaime. **Solitarios.** Barcelona: Bruguera, 1977. 187p.
(Bruguera bolsillo club). $E.
Contains a selection of solitaire card games.

Verdejo, Carmiña. **101 juegos de cartas: baraja española y
extranjera.** Barcelona: Sopena, 1975. 207p. (Biblioteca Sopena). HB. $C.
Provides fairly complete description of card games.

796—SPORTS

Diagram Group. **Gran libro de los deportes.** Madrid: Alce,
1976. 320p. HB. $A.
Translation of **Rules of the Game.** A well-illustrated,
handy reference tool describing how to play many sports.

796.332—American Football

*Cubillas, Francisco R. **Fútbol americano, fundamentos.** México: Trillas, 1982. 154p. $E.
The basics of American football.

796.334—Soccer

Escartín, Pedro. **Los mundiales que he vivido y el Mundial
'82.** Madrid: Paraninfo, 1981. 232p. $D.
The story of the World Soccer Championships from their
origin to the 1982 games. Written by a well-known Spanish
referee.

Fútbol. Barcelona: Aura, 1976. 48p. (Conozca el juego). $E.
A well-illustrated book on the rules and techniques of
soccer. This series is a translation of the British series
Know the Game. Other titles are: **Submarinismo** (scuba di-
ving), **Gimnasia** (gymnastics), **Baloncesto** (basketball), **Ba-
lonmano** (handball), **Patinaje** (roller and ice skating), **Bi-
llar** (billiards), **Boxeo** (boxing), **Tenis de mesa** (table ten-
nis).

Inglis, Simón. **Fútbol: habilidades, trucos y tácticas.**
   Madrid: PLESA, 1982. 31p. $E.
A well-illustrated, high-interest format book on soccer.
Will especially appeal to younger readers.

796.357—Baseball

Athletic Institute. **Mejore su béisbol.** México: Pax-
   México, 1968. 114p. $E.
This baseball title belongs to a sports collection
translated from a 1960 American series, published by the
Athletic Institute of Chicago. Photographs illustrate
techniques step by step. Some popular titles are: **Pista y
campo** (track and field), **Técnicas de salvamento** (lifesaving
techniques), **Mejore su natación** (swimming), **Mejore su
basquetbol** (basketball), **Mejore su lucha libre** (wrestling).

796.6—Cycling

Wilcockson, John. **Guía práctica de la bicicleta.** Madrid:
   Blume, 1982. 191p. $B.
Translation of **Bicycle: The Total Illustrated Guide to
Bicycles and Bicycling.** A well-illustrated book covering
the history, selection, and maintenance of bicycles. Also
discusses bicycle touring.

796.8153—Karate

Allred, Sam H. **Karate para adolescentes con técnicas de
   Kung Fu.** México: Mexicanos Unidos, 1975. 167p. $E.
This translation of **Karate for Teenagers** is a frequently
requested title. Written by a well-known karate instructor.

Nakayama, Masatoshi. **El mejor karate.** México: Diana, 1980.
   149p. $D.
Translation of **The Best Karate.** Large format,
well-illustrated title on the techniques of karate.

800 Literature and Rhetoric

808—RHETORIC AND COLLECTIONS

*Keithley, Erwin M., and Philip J. Schreiner, **Manual para la elaboración de tesis, monografías e informes.** Cincinnati: Southwestern, 1980. 107p.

A very useful handbook on all the technicalities of preparing theses, monographs, and reports. Includes a wealth of bibliographic and directory information on Spanish American sources.

808.6—Rhetoric of Letters

Allipandri, J. R. **Cómo se escribe una carta eficáz.** Barcelona: De Vecchi, 1975. 190p. $E.

A short, general handbook on letter writing, both business and personal.

Loury, Jean-Marie. **Cómo redactar sus cartas en 10 lecciones.** México: Diana, 1981. 175p. $D.

Offers suggestions on writing social, business, and personal correspondence. Includes samples.

Mata, P. M. **El gran libro de la moderna correspondencia comercial y privada.** Barcelona: De Vecchi, 1980. 285p. $C.

A handbook of both personal and commercial correspondence; includes a large number of examples.

808.81—Collections of Poetry

Algara, Julio. **Antología de poesías a la madre.** México:
Pax-México, 1975. $E.
This collection of poetry about mothers is especially
popular just before Mexican Mother's Day, May 10.

Antología de la poesía amorosa universal. México: Mexicanos
Unidos, 1979. 198p. $E.
A selection of romantic poetry, with emphasis on works
by Spanish authors.

*Zambrana, Carlos. **El declamador sin maestro.** 3. ed. México: Mexicanos Unidos, 1979. 207p. $E.
Gives basic techniques for public speaking, and includes
poems for dramatic presentations.

808.88—Quotations, Epigrams, Anecdotes

Escandon, Rafael. **Frases célebres para toda ocasión.** México: Diana, 1982. 282p. $E.
This selection is international and is arranged by subjects such as friendship, faith, history, etc.

809—History of Literature

*Pérez, Ramón D. **Literatura universal.** Barcelona: Sopena,
1971. 985p. (Biblioteca Hispania Ilustrada). HB. $C.
A general history of world literature from ancient to
modern times. Includes a listing of major literary prize
winners.

822.3—SHAKESPEARE

*Shakespeare, William. **Hamlet, La fierecilla domada, A
vuestro gusto, El rey Lear.** México: Porrúa, 1981.
224p. (Sépan cuantos, 94). $D.
Shakespeare's major plays are available in this good
paperback edition. Two additional volumes in the series are
nos. 96 and 86.

Shakespeare, William. **Hamlet, Penas por amor perdidas, Los
dos hidalgos de Verona, Sueño de una noche de verano,**

Romeo y Julieta. México: Porrúa, 1981. 272p. (Sépan cuantos, 86). $D.

*Shakespeare, William. **Macbeth, El mercader de Venecia. Las alegres comadres de Windsor, Julio César, La tempestad.** México: Porrúa, 1981. 248p. (Sépan cuantos, 96). $D.

851—ITALIAN POETRY

Dante, Alighieri. **La divina comedia.** Barcelona: Sopena, 1982. 684p. (Biblioteca Sopena). $E.
Translation of the great classic of Italian literature **The Divine Comedy.**

860—SPANISH LITERATURE

Bleiberg, Germán, ed. **Antología de la literatura española de los siglos XI al XVI.** Madrid: Alianza, 1976. 423p. $D.

Bleiberg, Germán, ed. **Antología de la literatura española del siglo XVI a mediados del XVII.** Madrid: Alianza, 1979. 327p. $D.

Bleiberg, Germán, ed. **Antología de la literatura española de mediados del siglo XVII a mediados del siglo XVIII.** Madrid: Alianza, 1980. 434p. $C.
An ongoing anthology of Spanish literature. These three volumes contain works from the 11th century to the middle of the 18th. Comprehensive, with a large number of entries of poetry, fiction, and drama. Contains useful, short introductions to authors and literary works. Reasonably priced.

Breve historia de la literatura española en su contexto. Madrid: Playor, 1981. 874p. $C.
A highly recommended survey of Spanish and Spanish American literature from its beginnings to the present. Includes a parallel history of Spanish arts and culture, with indexing and chronologies of literature, history, arts, and sciences.

García Lopez, José. **Historia de la literatura española.** Barcelona: Vicens-Vives, 1980. 708p. $A.

A good, general history of Spanish literature from its earliest beginnings to the 1950s. Periodically updated.

Río, Angel del, and Amelia Agostini del Río, comps. **Antología general de la literatura española: verso, prosa, teatro.** New York: Holt, 1960. 2v. HB.
A standard anthology of Spanish literature. Used by students, it is well organized and has good introductions to authors, periods, genres, etc. Does not include recent works.

860.8—Spanish American Literature

Anderson Imbert, Enrique, and Eugenio Florit. **Literatura hispanoamericana antología e introducción histórica.** New York: Holt, 1970. 2v.
A good, general anthology of Spanish American literature from its beginnings to modern times, with useful comments on the texts.

*Baudot, Georges. **Las letras precolombinas.** México: Siglo Veintiuno, 1979. 291p.
A basic anthology of pre-Columbian Indian literatures (Aztec, Maya, Inca), useful as an introduction to the subject. Translated from the French **Les lettres precolombiénnes.**

Colon Zayas, Eliseo. **Literatura del Caribe, antología, siglos XIX y XX.** Madrid: Playor, 1984. 418p. $B.
An excellent anthology of the literature Puerto Rico and Cuba of the 19th and 20th centuries. Includes biographical sketches.

Franco, Jean. **Historia de la literatura Hispanoamericana.** 2. ed. Barcelona: Ariel, 1979. 480p. $C.
A history of Spanish American literature from independence to the present. Arranged by literary genres, it supplements the Lazo title. Translated from English.

*Lazo, Raimundo. **Historia de la literatura hispanoamericana.** México: Porrúa, 1974-76. 2v. (Sépan cuantos, 38 and 65). $D.
A basic history of Spanish American literature from 1492 to 1914. Arranged by area and country, with a bibliography and indexes.

León-Portilla, Miguel. **Literatura del México antiguo.** Caracas: Biblioteca Ayacucho, 1978. 461p. $B.

Anthology of the ancient Indian literatures (Aztec, Maya) of Mexico. With introductions, versions, and chronology by an expert on the subject.

*Marco, Joaquín. **La nueva voz de un continente.** Barcelona: Salvat, 1982. 64p. (Colección Salvat, Temas Clave). HB. $E.
An excellent short survey of modern Spanish American literature, with special emphasis on the novel and its recent surge to prominence in world literature. Up-to-date and informative; useful for reference purposes and for introducing the layperson to the subject.

861—SPANISH AND SPANISH AMERICAN POETRY

Boccanera, Jorge, comp. **La novísima poesía latinoamericana.** México: Mexicanos Unidos, 1980. 310p. $D.
Presents the very recent generation of Latin American poets. Arranged by country of origin, with biographical notations. Useful, up-to-date work.

Conde Obregón, Ramón, comp. **Antología de la poesía española; de los primitivos a nuestros días.** 3. ed. Madrid: Auriga, 1979. 156p. (Nuevo Auriga). HB. $D.
An attractive selection of Spanish poetry, with a special appeal to young adults. Includes very short biographical information on each poet.

Crespo, Angel, comp. **Antología de la poesía modernista.** Tarragona, Spain: Tarraco, 1980. 347p. (Colección Arboli).
A representative anthology with a critical introduction to the poetry of the modernist movement, a great revival in Spanish poetry that spans the end of the 19th century to the 1930s.

Gaos, Vicente, comp. **Diez siglos de poesía castellana.** Madrid: Alianza, 1979. 496p. $D.
An anthology of Spanish poetry from the earliest times to mid-century. Includes biographical notes on individual poets.

García Rodríguez, Alfonso, and Angel García Aller, comps. **Antología de poetas hispanoamericanos contemporáneos.** León, Spain: Nebrija, 1980. 335p. $D.

An anthology of contemporary Spanish American poetry. Supplements the Crespo and Quiroga anthologies.

Gefaell, María Luisa. **El Cid.** Illustrated by Laszlo Gal. Barcelona: Noguer, 1970. 135p. $D.
The life and philosophy of the 12th century Spanish knight, Don Rodrigo Díaz de Vivar, is magnificently illustrated in this handsome adaptation of the famous Spanish epic poem.

*Guido, José. **Poesías populares.** New York: Ecuabooks, 1979. 186p. $C.
Has some of the most requested poems, and is especially good for locating special poems for Mother's Day and other holidays.

*Hernández, José. **Martin Fierro.** Buenos Aires: Sigmar, 1963. 150p.
Written for young adults, this is a condensed version of the well-known poem. Includes short, explanatory notes of words and phrases that are difficult to understand.

*Ibargoyen, Saúl, and Jorge Boccanera, comps. **La nueva poesía amorosa de América Latina.** México: Mexicanos Unidos, 1980. 347p. $D.
Love poetry by the young generation of Latin America poets. Arranged by country, with short biographies of poets. A very popular title.

Medina, Arturo, ed. **El silbo del aire--antología lírica infantil.** Barcelona: Vicens-Vives, 1971. 2v. 136p. $D ea.
Contains beautiful illustrations of narrative poems for young readers. Some of the authors represented are García Lorca, Juan Ramón Jiménez, Antonio Machado, and Gabriela Mistral.

*Montes de Oca, Francisco, comp. **Ocho siglos de poesía en lengua española.** México: Porrúa, 1978. 554p. (Sépan cuantos, 8). $D.
A good anthology of both Spanish and Spanish American poetry from the earliest times to the present, with short biographical information on the poets.

Montes de Oca, Francisco, comp. **Poesía mexicana.** México: Porrúa, 1968. 431p. (Sépan cuantos, 102). $D.
An excellent selection of the great poetry of Mexico. Includes brief biobibliographical sketches for each author represented.

Morales, Jorge Luis, comp. **Poesía afroantillana y negrista (Puerto Rico, Republica Dominicana, Cuba)**. 2. rev. ed. Río Piedras, P.R.: Universitaria, 1981. 456p.
New edition of a basic anthology of "negrista" poetry (poetry of the black experience) from three countries with an Afroantillean heritage: Puerto Rico, the Dominican Republic, and Cuba. Arranged by country, with short biographical notes and a glossary.

*Quiroga, Alfredo, comp. **Cien años de poesía hispano americana**. Barcelona: Bruguera, 1974. 572p. $E.
Anthology of Spanish American poetry from independence (ca.1820) to the beginning of the 20th century. Major poets are arranged chronologically according to poetic movements. Includes some explanatory text.

Individual Authors

The following is a chronological list of major poets from Spain (medieval to modern) and Spanish America (colonial to modern). Individual titles are listed only if they have special significance. Most works are available in a variety of editions, including paperback. Full bibliographic information has been included when a major work is mentioned.

Spain

***Poema de Mio Cid** (also **Cantar del Cid**) (ca.1140). Parts of Spain's great medieval epic is often included in anthologies of Spanish literature. It is also available in different editions, including paperbacks (e.g., Barcelona: Bruguera, 1978. 448p. $E).
San Juán de la Cruz (Saint John of the Cross) (1542-1591). Spain's greatest mystic poet.
Luis de Góngora y Argote (1561-1627). Famous for his rich baroque style and beautiful sonnets.
Francisco de Quevedo y Villegas (1580-1645). A great poet famous for his satirical poems. Author of the picaresque novel, **El buscón** (Madrid: Susaeta, 1976. 128p. $E).
*Gustavo Adolfo Becquer (1836-1870). Spain's greatest romantic poet. **Rimas**, also known as **Rimas y leyendas** (Barcelona: Bruguera, 1978. 420p. $E), includes his popular legends in prose.
Rosalia de Castro (1837-1885). Spain's greatest woman poet, who wrote beautiful poems on nature and man's destiny. In Spanish and Gallego.

Antonio Machado (1875-1939). A major modern poet, famous for his descriptive poems.
Juán Ramón Jiménez (1881-1958). A major lyric poet of deep personal emotions.
Pedro Salinas (1891-1951). Noted Spanish poet.
Jorge Guillén (b.1893). Contemporary famous poet.
*Federico García Lorca (1898-1936). Probably the best known poet of Spain, also famous for his plays. Works include **Romancero gitano** (gypsy ballads) and **Poemas del cante jondo** (Madrid: Cátedra, 1977. 320p. $E).
Vicente Aleixandre (b.1900). Nobel prize winner. Famous modern Spanish poet.
Rafael Alberti (b.1903). Contemporary Spanish poet.

Spanish America

*Sor Juana Inés de la Cruz (1651-1695). This 17th century Mexican nun is considered the greatest poet of the colonial period in Spanish America. Her **Obras completas** (collected works) is available in a good paperback edition (México: Porrúa, 1981. 984p. [Sépan cuantos, 100]).
José Hernández (1834-1886). Author of the famous narrative poem **Martin Fierro** (Buenos Aires: Centro Editor, 1979. 128p. $E), Argentina's national epic on gaucho (cowboy) life in the Pampa region.
José Martí (1853-1898). The great Cuban patriot was also an outstanding poet. Love and friendship are recurrent themes in his poetry, which includes the work, **Versos sencillos.** (México: Porrúa, 1982. 224p. [Sépan cuantos, 236]. $E).
*Rubén Darío (1867-1916). This famous poet from Nicaragua inspired the great revival of Hispanic poetry at the end of the 19th century. His works include **Azul** and **Cantos de vida y esperanza. (Páginas escogidas.** Madrid: Cátedra, 1979. 256p. $E.)
Amado Nervo (1870-1919). Mexican poet whose beautiful verse expresses the presence of death and love. Composed **Serenidad. (Antología.** México: Oasis, 1980. 222p. $E).
Gabriela Mistral, pseud. (Lucila Godoy de Alcayaga) (1889-1957). Famous Chilean poet and Nobel prize winner. Noted for her beautiful poems on the child and mother. Poems include **Desolación, Ternura, Tala,** and **Lagar** (México: Porrúa, 1979. 251p. [Sépan cuantos]. $E).
César Vallejo (1892-1938). A great Peruvian poet who wrote poems of exceptional purity and depth. Author of **Trilce** and **Poemas humanos. (Obra poética completa.** Caracas: Biblioteca Ayacucho, 1980. 420p. $C.)

Luis Palés Matos (1898-1958). A famous Puerto Rican poet,
best known for his poems inspired by the Afro-Puerto
Rican heritage. Works include **Tuntún de pasa· y gri-
fería**. (**Poesía completa y prosa selecta**. Caracas:
Biblioteca Ayacucho, 1978. 432p. $D)
Nicolás Guillén (b.1902). Cuban poet famous for his
sonorous poems inspired by the Afro-Cuban folk
tradition. Wrote **Sóngoro cosongo** (Madrid: Alianza,
1981. 366p. $E).
*Pablo Neruda, pseud. (Neftali Reyes) (1904-1973). This
Chilean poet and Nobel prize winner is one of the
greatest poets of Spanish America. Noted for his great
odes and beautiful love poems. Wrote **Veinte poemas de
amor y una canción desesperada** and **Odas elementales**.
(**Antología poética**. Madrid: Alianza, 1981. 560p. v.
I and II. $E ea.).
Manuel de Cabrál (b.1907). Outstanding contemporary poet of
the Dominican Republic. Wrote **Compadre Mon**, an epic
poem about the Dominican campesino.
Octavio Paz (b.1914). Mexico's greatest living poet. Wrote
both **Libertad bajo palabra** and **Salamandra**. (**Poemas
1935-1975**. Barcelona: Seix Barral, ía completa y prosa
selecta. Caracas: Biblioteca Ayacucho, 1978. 432p.
$D)
Julia de Burgos (1914-1953). A modern Puerto Rican poet,
who wrote some poetry that is universally considered
great. **Río grande de Loiza** is generally recognized as
her greatest piece.

862—SPANISH AND SPANISH AMERICAN DRAMA

Luzuriaga, Gerardo, and Richard Reeve, eds. **Los clásicos
del teatro hispanoamericano**. México: Fondo de Cultura
Económica, 1975. 908p.
     An anthology of the Spanish-American theater from its
origins to 1900, with biographical information on the
authors.

MacCurdy, Raymond, ed. **Spanish Drama of the Golden Age:
Twelve Plays**. New York: Irvington, 1979.
     A basic anthology of representative Spanish plays of the
16th and 17th centuries, the great age of the classical
Spanish theater with introductory texts in English.
Includes a basic bibliography.

Saz, Agustín del. **Teatro social hispanoamericano.** Barcelona: Labor, 1968. 178p. $D.
A good, basic history of the contemporary socially oriented Spanish-American theater. Discusses some of the best dramatic works from the area.

Solórzano, Carlos. **El teatro hispanoamericano contemporáneo.** México: Fondo de Cultura Económica, 1975. 2v. $D.

Teatro español contemporáneo: Benavente... México: Porrúa, 1979. 333p. (Sépan cuantos, 325). HB. $D.

Teatro español contemporáneo: López Rubio... México: Porrúa, 1977. 438p. (Sépan cuantos, 330). HB. $D.
These two anthologies contain 17 representative plays by major dramatic authors of the 20th century.

Teatro romántico. 2. ed. Barcelona: Bruguera, 1979. 784p. $E.
An anthology of 19th century romantic plays.

863—FICTION AND SHORT STORY COLLECTIONS

Bioy Casares, Adolfo, and Jorge Luis Borges, comps. **Los mejores cuentos policiales.** Madrid: Alianza, 1981. 329p. (El libro de bolsillo). $D.
A selection of some of the best detective stories in world literature, compiled by two very famous Spanish American authors.

Fernández Santos, Jesús, comp. **Siete narradores de hoy.** Madrid: Taurus, 1975. 190p. $D.
Contains 20 contemporary Spanish short stories by seven representative Spanish authors.

*La novela picaresca. 3. ed. Madrid: Taurus, 1967. 589p. HB. $D.
Includes major works of the picaresque genre (early Spanish fiction), such as **La Celestina, El lazarillo de Tormes, Guzmán de Alfarache, El Buscón,** etc.

*Seymour, Menton, ed. **El cuento hispanoamericano, antología crítico-histórica.** México: Fondo de Cultura Económica, 1974. 2v.

An excellent collection of some of the best examples of the short story in Spanish American literature, with biographical introductions to the authors. Each story is followed by a critical commentary. Includes a bibliography.

863—Spanish Fiction

The following is a selection of works from the second half of the 19th century to the present. Representative works of the early Spanish novel, which belong mostly to the picaresque genre, are included in the anthology **La novela picaresca**, listed above. For selecting recent fiction, check the winners of Spain's major literary prizes, such as the Cervantes (national prize), Nadal, and Planeta.

*Alarcón, Pedro Antonio de. **El sombrero de tres picos.** Barcelona: Bruguera, 1982. 160p. HB. $D.
This short novel on how a miller's wife outwits her high-ranking suitor is noted for its light humor and lively style.

Alas, Leopoldo (pseud. Clarín). **La Regenta.** Barcelona: Bruguera, 1982. 800p. HB. $D.
A late 19th century novel describing events in Oviedo. It centers on the unhappy love life of its heroine, La Regenta.

*Baroja, Pío. **Camino de perfección.** Madrid: Caro Raggio, 1972. 335p. $E.
The adventurous life of this novel's hero, Fernando Osorio, unfolds against the background of Spanish cities and countryside. A good example of this great, prolific novelist's very readable style.

Blasco Ibañez, Vicente. **Sangre y arena.** Barcelona: Plaza & Janés, 1977. 320p. $E.
A bullfighter's rise to fame and fortune, and his tragic end are the subject of this novel by a famous early 20th-century novelist.

Caballero, Fernán, pseud. (Bohl de Faber, Cecilia). **La Gaviota.** Barcelona: Bruguera, 1981. 320p. HB. $D.
A country girl, after rising to fame as a singer in Sevilla, betrays her husband to whom she owes everything. After he leaves her, she loses fame and fortune, and dies in obscurity. A 19th century romantic novel.

Castillo Puche, José Luis. **Hicieron partes.** Barcelona: Destino, 1967. 326p. $E.
A Spanish businessman's greed in building a fortune results in tragic events. Set in Spain at the time of the Civil War.

*Cela, Camilo José. **La familia de Pascual Duarte.** Barcelona: Destino, 1982. 176p. $E.
The story of a tragic family relationship that ends in murder. Set in a poverty-stricken Spanish village, this book is by one of the best modern Spanish writers.

*Cervantes Saavedra, Miguel de. **El ingenioso hidalgo Don Quijote de la Mancha.** 19. ed. México: Porrúa, 1979. 692p. (Sépan cuantos, 6).
Tells about the wonderful adventures of the errant knight, Don Quijote, and his faithful follower. A major classic in world literature. This reasonably priced edition includes an introduction, a biographical sketch of the author, and indexes to names and events that appear in the text. (For a good, basic interpretation of Don Quijote, see Martín de Riquer, **Aproximación al Quijote.** Barcelona: Teide, 1976. 236p. HB. $E.)

Delibés, Miguel. **Cinco horas con Mario.** Barcelona: Destino, 1981. 296p. $D.
A woman reflects on her past after the funeral of her former husband. This work focuses on how reality is distorted by false values and conventions.

Fernández Flórez, Darío. **Lola, espejo oscuro.** Barcelona: Plaza & Janés, 1977. 448p. $E.
Humorous presentation of the seamy side of city life, revealed through the adventures of a prostitute.

García Hortelano, Juan. **Tormenta de verano.** Barcelona: Argos Vergara, 1977. 352p. $E.
A young woman is found dead on a desolate beach. The mystery that develops is written with exceptionally fine psychological insight.

*García Pavón, Francisco. **Las hermanas coloradas.** Barcelona: Destino, 1972. 209p. $D.
Plimio, the Spanish Sherlock Holmes, solves a mystery related to two sisters in Madrid. This detective story is one of several with Plimio as the protagonist.

Gironella, José María. **Los cipreses creen en Dios.** Barcelona: Planeta, 1981. 768p. $D.

The first novel in the author's famous trilogy on the Spanish Civil War, which gives a vivid picture not only of Spain but also of Europe turning to totalitarianism on the eve of World War II.

Goytisolo, Juán. **Fiestas**. Barcelona: Destino, 1977. 238p. $D.
Excellent depiction of life in a big city slum, revolving around outcasts on the margins of society.

*Jiménez, Juan Ramón. **Platero y yo**. Barcelona: Bruguera, 1982. 304p. $D.
The charming story of Platero, the little donkey, told by his friend, the poet. This work, by one of Spain's greatest modern poets, is a classic with special young adult appeal.

Laforet, Carmen. **Nada**. Barcelona: Destino, 1979. 296p. $E.
An adolescent's discovery of the adult world reveals disintegrating lower middle class values. By an outstanding novelist.

*Laiglesia, Alvaro de. **Tu también naciste desnudito**. Barcelona: Planeta, 1971. $E.
A satire of contemporary society presented through humorous descriptions of a series of daily events. The author is one of the best-known writers of light, humorous novels and short stories. All his writings are recommended.

Lera, Angel María de. **Las últimas banderas**. Barcelona: Planeta, 1981. 336p. $E.
One of the best novels on the Civil War of 1936-1939; possesses outstanding narrative qualities reminiscent of Hemingway.

Luca de Tena, Torcuato. **La mujer de otro**. Barcelona: Planeta, 1980. 288p. $D.
A novel on marital infidelity, presenting a fine analysis of its moral and social implications.

*Madariaga, Salvador de. **El corazón de piedra verde**. Madrid: Espasa-Calpe, 1981. 646p. $B.
A major historical trilogy on the Spanish conquest of Mexico. The series consists of **Los fantasmas, Los dioses sanguinarios, Fe sin blasfemia**, and is written by an internationally known Spanish intellectual.

Marse, Juan. **Ultimas tardes con Teresa.** Barcelona: Bruguera, 1981. 416p. $E.
The romantic love story of a young man from the slums
and the daughter of upper middle-class parents.

Martínez Ruiz, José (pseud. Azorín). **Doña Inés.** Madrid:
Castalia, 1981. 256p. $E.
This love story of Doña Inés and Diego, set in 19th century Spain, is noted for its descriptive qualities. By one
of the greatest masters of the Spanish language.

Matute, Ana María. **Fiesta al noroeste.** Madrid: Cátedra,
1978. 168p. $E.
A story of human passions played out in a rural setting
and centering on a repulsive local potentate.

Palacio Valdes, Armando. **La hermana San Sulpicio.** México:
Porrúa, 1980. 212p. (Sépan cuantos, 212). $E.
The love story of a nun and a young doctor who marry
after she leaves the convent. Set in the traditional atmos-
phere of southern Spain.

Palou, Inés. **Carne apaleada.** Barcelona: Planeta, 1980.
224p. $D.
This powerful novel describing life in a women's prison
is based on the author's personal experiences.

Pardo Bazán, Emilia. **Los Pazos de Ulloa.** Barcelona:
Bruguera: 1981. $E.
This famous naturalistic novel describes tragic events
in a rural mansion in the Galicia region at the end of the
19th century.

Pérez de Ayala, Ramón. **Tigre Juan.** Madrid: Castalia, 1980.
346p. $E.
The classical Spanish theme of Don Juan, the conqueror
of women's hearts, is played out in a traditional Spanish
provincial town. Written by a major novelist of the first
half of the century.

*Pérez Galdós, Benito. **Doña Perfecta.** México: Porrúa,
1981. 314p. (Sépan cuantos, 107). $D.
Portrayal of a domineering woman whose prejudices and
bigotry result in the murder of an innocent person. By one
of Spain's greatest novelists, whose works include
individual titles from his great historical series **Episodios
nacionales** (Madrid: Alianza, 1976. 46v. $A).

Quiroga, Elena.   **La sangre.**   Barcelona: Destino, 1981.
    348p. $E.
This is the story of four generations of a Spanish family. The link between the family members is a tree, which
has provided a protective shade for all.

Salisachs, Mercedes.   **La presencia.**   Barcelona: Argos
    Vergara, 1982. 304p. $D.
The fine psychological workings of intimate human relations are revealed in the course of a few hours in this novel, one of the latest by a popular and prolific writer.

Salvador, Tomás.   **Un lugar llamado lejos.**   Barcelona: Plaza
    & Janés, 1979. 272p. HB. $C.
The conversations of an elderly man and a small girl re-
veal the hidden poetry of life. The author's identification
with the young and the unfortunate give his writing a
special appeal.

Sender, Ramón.   **Epitalamio del prieto Trinidad.**   Barcelona:
    Destino, 1973. 304p. $D.
The story of a revolt in a penal colony in the Caribbean
area. A profound exploration of the disturbing aspects of
violence. The author is a major contemporary novelist.

Umbral, Francisco.   **Mortal y rosa.**   Barcelona: Destino,
    1979. 195p. $E.
Reflections on dying form the central theme of this nov-
el, which has been translated into English as **A Mortal
Spring.**

*Unamuno, Miguel de.   **Abel Sánchez.**   Madrid: Espasa-Calpe,
    1980. 150p. $E.
A family hatred that culminates in fratricide is the
subject of this novel by a very famous Spanish writer. Additional novels of importance are **La tia Tula** and **Niebla.**

Valera, Juan.   **Pepita Jiménez.**   Madrid: Espasa-Calpe, 1980.
    304p. $D.
A charming rural love story by a major 19th century novelist.

*Valle-Inclán, Ramón del.   **Sonata de primavera.**   Barcelona:
    Bruguera, 1981. 160p. $E.
Part of famous novel series, usually included in one
volume, named for the four seasons. This series revolves
around the romantic and somewhat eccentric figure of the
Marqués de Brandomín, who is described in the author's exquisite style.

Vásquez Figueroa, Alberto. **Como un perro rabioso.** Barcelona: Plaza & Janés, 1975. 128p. $D.
Story of the life-and-death struggle of an escaped political prisoner in Central America and a pursuing attack dog. Receved the Planeta literary prize for 1979.

Vázquez Montalban, Manuel. **Los mares del sur.** Barcelona: Planeta, 1981. 232p. $D.
This seemingly conventional mystery develops into a profound social and psychological investigation. Winner of the Planeta literary prize for 1979.

Zunzunegui, Juan Antonio de. **Las ratas del barco.** Barcelona: Noguer, 1968. 348p. $E.
The suspenseful story of a family where evil and good are represented in a series of characters. By a prolific contemporary novelist.

863.8—Latin American Fiction

Alegría, Ciro. **El mundo es ancho y ajeno.** Madrid: Alianza, 1982. 624p. $D.
Published in 1941, this is one of the best "indianistas" novels in Latin America. The work is a social protest concerning an Indian town, Rumi, which is destroyed by the greediness of white men. The Peruvian author was imprisoned and later exiled because of his political beliefs.

Arenas, Reynaldo. **Termina el desfile.** Barcelona: Seix Barral, 1981. 174p. $D.
One of the most brilliant of the younger generation of Cuban writers, the author was the recipient of a Guggenheim Fellowship in 1981. This novel presents a social picture of life in Cuba.

Arévalo Martíez, Rafael. **El hombre que parecía un caballo.** San José, Costa Rica: Educa, 1970. 154p. $E.
The author, who introduced the "psico-zoological" story in Latin America, here presents a game of the imagination, showing the likeness in soul and body between humans and animals.

Argüedas, Alcides. **Raza de bronce.** Buenos Aires: Losada, 1957. 247p. $D.
The most famous of the Bolivian writer's novels and the first contemporary novel written about the Indians. Published in 1919.

Argüedas, José María. **Los ríos profundos.** Madrid: Alianza, 1981. 256p. $D.
This Peruvian novelist and folklorist wrote both in Spanish and Quechua. This most famous of his novels is an Indian story set in the beautiful and gloomy violence of the Andes.

Arlt, Roberto. **Los siete locos.** Barcelona: Bruguera, 1980. 288p. $D.
This Argentinian novel deals with the author's unhappy childhood and adolescence. Published in 1929, this work was widely read in Buenos Aires, largely due to Arlt's focus on problems that were very real to the average person.

*Asturias, Miguel Angel. **El Señor Presidente.** Madrid: Alianza, 1981. 312p. $D.
The Guatemalan author was the winner of the 1967 Nobel Prize for literature and the 1966 Lenin Prize. This novel describes life under the dictatorship of Estrada Cabrera, but its theme is universal.

Azuela, Mariano. **Los de abajo.** Madrid: Cátedra, 1980. 224p. $E.
This Mexican author is a spokesman for the oppressed and one of the most important writers of the Mexican Revolution. Published in 1915, this is the most read and most translated Mexican novel of all times.

Benedetti, Mario. **Montevideanos.** México: Nueva Imágen, 1980. 152p. $E.
Contains excellent short stories that depict the life of ordinary people in Uruguay. Published in 1955, it won the Premio Municipal de Literatura in 1959.

Benedetti, Mario. **La tregua.** Madrid: Cátedra, 1982. 264p. $E.
Published in 1960, this novel is based on a true story about the marriage of a man in his fifties to a very young girl. Winner of the Premio Nacional de Literatura in 1960.

Blest Gana, Alberto. **Martin Rivas.** Madrid: Cátedra, 1981. 464p. $D.
The founder of the novel in Chile, this well-known author writes about the life and customs in Chilean society around 1851.

Bombal, María Luisa. **La última niebla.** Santiago: Andina, 1970. 185p. $D.

This Chilean novel, published in 1935, is a subjective and sensual work. It takes the reader into the world of dreams.

Bosch, Juan. **Cuentos escritos en el exilio.** Santo Domingo: Dominicana, 1971. $D.
A collection of short stories by one of the strongest opponents of Trujillo's dictatorship. The author was exiled from the Dominican Republic in 1937.

Bryce Echenique, Alfredo. **Un mundo para Julius.** Barcelona: Seix Barral, 1970. 591p. $D.
The author's first novel, which shows the injustice of life to some people, portrays the happy and worry-free life of Julius, an intelligent child, fruit of the carefree oligarchy.

Cabrera Infante, Guillermo. **Tres tristes tigres.** Barcelona: Seix Barral, 1981. 456p. $E.
This novel is one of the most brilliant Cuban works ever written and won the Premio Biblioteca Breve. Published in 1964, it presents vignettes of Cuban life, painted in exquisite language.

Carpentier, Alejo. **El reino de este mundo.** Barcelona: Seix Barral, 1981. 150p. $E.
The Cuban author of this novel, published in 1949, recreates the period of King Henri Christophe of Haiti. Its style is that of the "realismo mágico" (magical realism).

Carpentier, Alejo. **El siglo de las luces.** Barcelona: Seix Barral, 1980. 372p. $E.
Based on real facts, this novel describes the adventures of Victor Hughes in the Caribbean Sea and, particularly, in Haiti.

Carrasquilla, Tomás. **La marquesa de Yolombó.** Bogotá: Caro y Cuervo, 1974. 630p. $D.
Set in the 18th century, this novel centers on a town in Antioquia, Colombia. Published in 1928.

*Castellanos, Rosario. **Balún-Canán.** México: Fondo de Cultura Económica, 1973. 292p. $D.
Published in 1957, this is an excellent example of a contemporary novel, especially in its theme and structure. It has been translated into English, French, and German. A poetic work of mystery and magic offering a view of Indian life, culture, and problems.

Cortázar, Julio. **Final del Juego.** Buenos Aires: Sudamericana, 1969. 195p. $D.
This is the Guatemalan author's third work, a collection
of stories.   In one story, "Axolotl," the protagonist be-
lieves that he is one of the monsters he sees in an aquarium.

Cortázar, Julio. **Rayuela.** Barcelona: Bruguera, 1981.
640p. $D.
This novel, published in 1963, is noted for its new and
original approach.   The author begins his work with a
"Tablero de direcciones" (set of directions), which explains
to the reader the way the novel should be read.

Donoso, José. **La misteriosa desaparición de la Marquesita
de Loria.** Barcelona: Seix Barral, 1981. 208p. $D.
Written by one of Chile's most famous contemporary writers, this is an erotic novel set in Madrid in the 1920s.

Donoso, José. **El obsceno pájaro de la noche.** Barcelona:
Seix Barral, 1981. 552p. $D.
This novel, published in 1970, is probably the Chilean
writer's most important work to date.   The protagonist and
narrator of this complex work becomes the "right hand" of an
influential politician.   His multiple identities, his fanta-
sies, and his distrust reflect the tragedies of modern man.

Edwards, Jorge. **Persona non grata.** Barcelona: Seix Barral,
1973. 398p. $D.
The novel describes the author's polemic and controversial mission to Havana as the first diplomat from Chile to
Castro's Cuba.

*Fuentes, Carlos. **La muerte de Artemio Cruz.** Barcelona:
Bruguera, 1982. 320p. $E.
Born in Mexico, Fuentes is one of a group of writers
reacting against the regionalism imposed by the Mexican
Revolution.   This novel, published in 1962, offers a vast
view of the Mexican society of his time.

Gallegos, Rómulo. **Doña Bárbara.** Barcelona: Círculo de Lectores, 1968. 348p. $E.
Written in 1929, this novel is one of the best in Latin
America. It portrays the confrontation between Doña Bárbara,
a countryman from the plains of Venezuela, and Santos Lu-
zardo, a lawyer who represents the life of the city.

*García Márquez, Gabriel. **Cien años de soledad.** Barcelona: Plaza & Janés, 1980. 384p. $D.
The favorite work of the author, this novel is based on a true incident and was not published until all the participants had died. His masterpiece.

Güiraldes, Ricardo. **Don Segundo Sombra.** Madrid: Cátedra: 1981. 320p. $E.
This Argentinian author won the Premio Nacional de Literatura for this novel written in 1926 in which he evokes and defends the gaucho. Although the work is based on a regional character, it has great universal value.

Guzmán, Martín Luis. **El águila y la serpiente.** México: General, 1970. 455p. $D.
Written by a Mexican journalist who took part in the Mexican Revolution. His books are more fact than fiction.

Hostos, Eugenio María de. **La peregrinación de Bayoán.** Barcelona: Vosgos, 1976. 120p. $E.
A political novel about the independence and union of the West Indies; published in 1863. The Puerto Rican author intended his writing to help mankind.

Icaza, Jorge. **Huasipungo.** Barcelona: Plaza & Janés, 1982. 192p. $E.
Published in 1934, this is an angry novel about the exploitation of the Indian peasants in Ecuador. The story centers on the construction of a road with the free labor of oppressed Indians.

*Isaacs, Jorge. **María.** Barcelona: Bruguera, 1976. 448p. $E.
A romantic story published in 1867. Considered the most representative work of the Romantic Period in Latin America.

Laguerre, Enrique. **La llamarada.** San Juan: Rumbos, 1968. 228p. $D.
Published in 1935, this is an intense and tragic account of the life of the oppressed jíbaro (peasant) in the cane fields of Puerto Rico.

Lezama Lima, José. **Paradiso.** Madrid: Cátedra, 1980. 656p. $E.
The author of this monumental artistic creation was hailed by the New York Times as "the Proust of the Spanish language." The novel, published in 1966, depicts the struggle of the protagonist to move away from homosexuality,

thematically representing the movement from anarchy to order.

Lynch, Benito. **El inglés de los guesos.** México: General, 1967. $D.
Published in 1924, this is the story of a tragic love affair between a beautiful gauchita and an English archaeologist. It is the most famous of the Argentinian writer's works.

Lynch, Benito. **Palo Verde.** Buenos Aires: Troquel, 1967. $E.
A fine study, published in 1925, of the different types of pamperos found in Argentina.

Mallea, Eduardo. **La bahía de silencio.** Buenos Aires: Sudamericana, 1978. $D.
This novel, published in 1940, contains very little dialogue, exemplifying the lack of communiçation in the world today. The Argentinian author is the recipient of many literary awards, and his work assimilates the new directions taken by the contemporary novel in Europe.

Mármol, José. **Amalia.** Barcelona: Sopena, 1978. 592p. $E.
Argentina's first novel, this is a political work denouncing the dictatorship of Juan Manuel Rosas, who ruled Argentina during the Romantic period.

Onetti, Juan Carlos. **El astillero.** Barcelona: Seix Barral, 1978. 222p. $D.
This study of the ambiguity of human conduct in today's world was written by one of Uruguay's most outstanding authors. It was published in 1978.

Otero Silva, Miguel. **Cuando quiero llorar no lloro.** Barcelona: Seix Barral, 1981. 200p. $E.
This Venezuelan novel depicts the effect the oil industry has on the lives of the common people and on the small towns.

Parra, Teresa de la. **Memorias de Mamá Blanca.** Salsaldella, Spain: Plon, 1979. 160p. $E.
Written by one of the best prose writers in Latin America, this beautiful novel recreates the author's childhood and the people who filled it.

Poniatowska, Elena. **Hasta no verte, Jesus mío.** México: Era, 1981. 315p. $C.

Published in 1969, this novel is about the life of a simple Mexican woman who lives through the Mexican Revolution.

Puig, Manuel. **Pubis angelical.** Barcelona: Seix Barral, 1982. 272p. $E.
Puig, an Argentinian, is one of the most popular Latin American authors. This 1979 novel, considered his masterwork, has two parallel stories, one imaginary and one true, about unfortunate love.

Quiroga, Horacio. **Cuentos de la selva.** México: Mexicanos Unidos, 1983. 118p. $E.
The author, born in Uruguay, is noted for the universality of his work. This collection of short stories published in 1918 is set amid barbarous nature, with the protagonists generally defeated by natural forces. Quiroga's stories are essentially morbid.

Revueltas, José. **En algún valle de lágrimas.** México: Era, 1979. 106p. $D.
A short novel, published in 1956, that focuses on a man who equates the right to private property with life itself.

*Rivera, José Eustasio. **La vorágine.** Madrid: Alianza, 1981. 188p. $E.
A novel, written in 1924, about the jungle and the confrontation between man and nature. Written by a native of Colombia, this is one of the best examples of the so-called super-regionalism in Latin America.

Roa Bastos, Augusto. **Hijo de hombre.** Barcelona: Círculo de Lectores, 1973. 296p. $E.
Written in 1959, this novel covers social and political life in Paraguay. The work is a passionate defense of human rights and a reproach of injustice, political dictatorship, prejudices, and social class abuses.

Rojas, Manuel. **Hijo de ladrón.** Barcelona: Bruguera, 1980. 288p. $E.
The author was the first to react against "costumbrismo" (social criticism) in Chile. In this novel, published in 1951, he presents the world of a thief--as seen by the average person, the American.

*Romero, José Rubén. **La vida inútil de Pito Pérez.** México: Porrúa, 1981. 232p. $D.
Picaresque novel published in 1938 in which its Mexican

author satirizes Mexican society of the post-revolutionary period.

*Rulfo, Juan. **El llano en llamas.** México: Fondo de Cultura Económica, 1981. 152p. $E.
Published in 1953, this work contains three books of short stories about the life, despair, anguish, and helplessness of the peasants. The work brought Rulfo both national and international recognition.

Rulfo, Juan. **Pedro Páramo.** México: Fondo de Cultura Económica, 1977. 128p. $E.
In this work, considered by many Rulfo's best, the dead and the living, past and present interact in a story about a family dealing with a cacique.

Sánchez, Luis Rafael. **La guaracha del Macho Camacho.** Barcelona: Vergara, 1982. 232p. $D.
This Puerto Rican novel, published in 1976, revolves around the "guaracha." Different characters, representing Puerto Rico's society, interlace their lives as if they were dancing with an ever present musical background.

Sarduy, Severo. **De dónde son los cantantes.** Barcelona: Seix Barral, 1980. 160p. $E.
Written by a well-known Cuban author, this novel presents the cyclical changes that took place when early Spain, Africa and Asia began exchanging ideas and cultural traits. It was published in 1967.

Scorza, Manuel. **La tumba del relámpago.** Madrid: Siglo XXI, 1981. 272p. $E.
This novel, which has been translated into several languages, deals with the true story of the struggle of the comunero (sharecroppers) in Peru to recover the lands taken from them by the rich landowners and foreign companies.

Uslar Pietri, Arturo. **Las lanzas coloradas.** Barcelona: Bruguera, 1981. 256p. $D.
Written by one of Venezuela's most important modern authors, this work covers the epic struggle of the Venezuelan people to achieve political independence. Published in 1931.

*Vargas Llosa, Mario. **La ciudad y los perros.** Barcelona: Seix Barral, 1982. 385p. $D.
Published in 1977, this novel denounces life in a Peruvian military academy--its brutality and the false

virility instilled in the students in an effort to form heroes. The narrative is realistic and passionate but is presented in an impersonal tone. Vargas Llosa is one of the leading Latin American contemporary novelists and his works are instant bestsellers.

Villaverde, Cirilo. **Cecilia Valdés** Barcelona: Vosgos, 1978. 300p. $E.
The author's great descriptive talent is evident in this, his best-known novel. Published in 1882, it portrays everyday life and customs in Cuba, and relates the love story of a beautiful mulata who falls in love with a white landowner who is also her half-brother.

Yañez, Agustin. **Al filo del agua.** México: Porrúa, 1982. 389p. $E.
This novel explores the collective conscience of a small town in Jalisco right before the revolution. Published in 1947, the story is set in Mexico at the height of the European influence.

863--Fiction in Spanish Translation

Given the vast amount of the fiction being translated from other languages into Spanish--both classics and popular works (bestsellers)--the following selective list should serve only as a reminder of what books a library providing good reading in Spanish would not want to miss. The unannotated listing is alphabetized by author.

Amado, Jorge. **Doña Flor y sus dos maridos.** Madrid: Alianza, 1981. 448p. $D.
The English title of this Portuguese original by the famous Brazilian novelist is **Doña Flor and Her Two Husbands.**

*Andersen, Hans Christian. **Cuentos de Andersen.** Barcelona: Bruguera, 1978. 223p. $E.
Contains fairy tales by the famous Danish storyteller.

Austen, Jane. **Orgullo y prejuicio.** Barcelona: Juventud, 1974. 240p. $E.
Translation of **Pride and Prejudice.**

Balzac, Honore de. **Eugenia Grandet.** Barcelona: Sopena, 1978. 224p. $E.
Translation of **Eugenie Grandet.**

*Brontë, Emily. **Cumbres borrascosas.**   Barcelona: Plaza &
Janés, 1978. 432p. $E
Translation of **Wuthering Heights.**

Camus, Albert.   **El extranjero.**   Madrid: Alianza, 1978.
144p. $E.
Translation of **The Stranger** (**L'etranger** in French).

*Defoe, Daniel.   **Robinson Crusoe.**   Barcelona: Sopena, 1975.
464p. $E.
Translation of the same English title.

Dickens, Charles.   **Grandes esperanzas.**   Barcelona: Bruguera,
1974. 576p. $E.
Translation of **Great Expectations.**

*Dostoyevski, Fédor.   **Crimen y castigo.**   Barcelona:
Bruguera, 1978. 672p. $E.
Translation of the great Russian novel **Crime and
Punishment.**

*Dumas, Alexandre.   **La dama de las camelias.**   Barcelona:
Bruguera, 1975. 336p. $E.
Translation of the famous French romantic novel **La Dame
aux Camelias.**

*Dumas, Alexandre.   **Tres mosqueteros.**   Barcelona: Bruguera,
1974. 319p. $E.
Translation of **The Three Musketeers.**

*Dumas, Alexandre.   **Veinte años después.**   Barcelona: Sopena,
1977. 718p. $E.
Translation of **Twenty Years After.**

Fielding, Henry.   **Tom Jones.**   Madrid: Promoción y Ediciones,
1978. 2v. $D.
Translation of the same English title.

Fitzgerald, F. Scott.   **El Gran Gatsby.**   Barcelona: Plaza
& Janés, 1977. 208p. $E.
Translation of **The Great Gatsby.**

*Flaubert, Gustave.   **Madame Bovary.**   Barcelona: Sopena,
1982. 272p. $E.
Translation of the same French title.

Gibran, Kahlil.   **El profeta.**   México: Libro-Mex, 1983.
194p. $E.

Gibran's aphorisms and parables are frequently requested in Spanish.

Hawthorne, Nathaniel. **La letra escarlata.** Madrid: Narcea, 1977. 406p. $E.
Translation of **The Scarlet Letter.**

Hemingway, Ernest. **Por quien doblan las campanas.** Barcelona: Planeta, 1981. 413p. $E.
Translation of **For Whom the Bells Toll.**

*Hugo, Victor. **Los miserables.** Barcelona: Sopena, 1977. 2v. $D.
Translation of the French title **Les miserables.**

*Huxley, Aldous. **Un mundo feliz.** Barcelona: Plaza & Janés, 1976. 320p. $E.
Translation of **Brave New World.**

*Joyce, James. **Ulises.** Barcelona: Lumen, 1976. 584p. $D.
Translation of **Ulysses.**

Mann, Thomas. **La montaña mágica.** Barcelona: Plaza & Janés, 1979. 2v. $D.
Translation of **The Magic Mountain.**

Manzoni, Alessandro. **Los novios.** Barcelona: Sopena, 1980. 535p. $E.
Translation of the famous Italian novel **I promessi sposi.**

*Mitchell, Margaret. **Lo que el viento se llevó.** Barcelona: Ayma, 1977. 1004p. $D.
Translation of **Gone With the Wind.**

*Pasternak, Boris. **El doctor Jivago.** Barcelona: Noguer, 1974. 448p. $E.
Translation of **Doctor Zhivago.**

Steinbeck, John. **Las uvas de la ira.** Barcelona: Planeta, 1978. 432p. $E.
Translation of **The Grapes of Wrath.**

Stevenson, Robert Louis. **El Dr. Jekill y Mr. Hyde.** Madrid: Alianza, 1981. 126p. $E.
Translation of **Dr. Jekyll and Mr. Hyde.**

Stevenson, Robert Louis. **La isla del tesoro**. Barcelona:
Bruguera, 1977. 255p. $E.
Translation of **Treasure Island**.

Swift, Jonathan. **Viajes de Gulliver**. Madrid: Bruguera,
1978. 223p. $E.
Translation of **Gulliver's Travels**.

*Tolstoi, Leo. **Guerra y paz**. Barcelona: Bruguera, 1978.
2v. HB. $C.
Translation of the famous Russian novel with the English
title **War and Peace**. Tolstoi's other great novel, **Anna
Karenina**, is also available in Spanish.

*Twain, Mark (pseud. for Samuel Langhorne Clemens).
Aventuras de Huck Finn. Barcelona: Sopena, 1982. 350p.
$E.
Translation of **The Adventures of Huckleberry Finn**.

Verne, Jules. **La vuelta al mundo en ochenta dias**.
Barcelona: Bruguera, 1977. 336p. $E.
Translation of **Around the World in 80 Days**.

Wilde, Oscar. **Cuentos de Oscar Wilde**. Madrid: Magisterio
Español, 1979. 208p. $E.
Translation of **Oscar Wilde's Tales**, which will have a
special appeal to young adults. Also worth reading is a
translation of Wilde's **Picture of Dorian Gray**, **Retrato de
Dorian Gray** (Barcelona: Bruguera, 1974. 336p. $E).

892.7—**Arabic Literature**

Arabian Nights. **Mil y una noches**. México: Porrúa, 1983.
369p. $D.

ADDITIONAL AUTHORS

Following is a list of authors whose most popular works
have been translated into Spanish and are available from
distributors of Spanish materials:

V. C. Andrews	Simone de Beauvoir	Madeleine Brent
Richard Bach	Saul Bellow	Emily Brontë
Vicki Baum	Peter Benchley	Pearl S. Buck

Erskine Caldwell
Taylor Caldwell
Truman Capote
Philippa Carr
Henri Charriere
Agatha Christie
James Clavell
Robin Cook
Avery Corman
Catherine Cookson
Dorothy Eden
Robert Elegant
Catherine Gaskin
Howard Fast
F. Scott
 Fitzgerald
Ken Follett
Frederick Forsyth
Ernest Gann
Erle S. Gardner
John Godey
William Goldmann
Andrew Greeley
Gerald Green
Zane Grey
Judith Guest
Arthur Hailey
Thomas Harris
Pat Highsmith

Alfred Hitchcock
Victoria Holt
Susan Howatch
John Irving
Rona Jaffe
John Jakes
Erica Jong
Stephen King
Jerzy Kosinsky
Judith Krantz
Dominique Lapierre
 (pseud. for
 Larry Collins)
John Le Carré
Doris Lessing
Ira Levin
Johanna Lindsey
Norah Lofts
Robert Ludlum
Peter Maas
Ross MacDonald
Alistair McLean
Patricia Matthews
William S. Maugham
Colleen McCullough
Herman Melville
James Michener
Anaïs Nin
George Orwell

Belva Plain
Mario Puzo
Harold Robbins
Rosemary Rogers
Phillip Roth
Lawrence Sanders
Erich Segal
Irwin Shaw
Sidney Sheldon
Danielle Steele
John Steinbeck
Jacqueline Susann
Barbara Taylor-
 Bradford
Thomas Thompson
Alvin Toffler
J. R. R. Tolkien
Leon Uris
Helen Van Slyke
Jules Verne
Erich Von Daniken
Irving Wallace
Joseph Wambaugh
Norris West
Phyllis Whitney
Kathleen
 Woodiwiss

900 General Geography, History, etc.

901—PHILOSOPHY AND THEORY OF HISTORY

Tuñón de Lara, Manuel. **¿Por qué la historia?** Barcelona: Salvat, 1981. 64p. (Temas clave). $E.
A discussion of the importance of history. Describes history as a science, the problems of objectivity, and how history is written. Very readable and well-illustrated treatment of a sometimes dry subject.

909—WORLD HISTORY

Rosello Moea, María. **5.000 años de historia.** Barcelona: Sopena, 1979. 689p. (Biblioteca Hispania Ilustrada). HB. $C.
A well-illustrated survey of world history from the earliest times to 1970.

Vera Tornell, Ricardo. **Historia universal de la civilización.** Barcelona: Sopena, 1974. 2v. HB. $B.
Adapted from the **Outlines of the World's History**, published by Cambridge University. This two-volume set covers the major civilizations from the beginning of history to the 20th century. Includes a section on the individual countries of Latin America.

910—GEOGRAPHY

*Geografía universal. Barcelona: Sopena, 1980.   599p.
(Biblioteca Hispania Ilustrada). HB. $C.
Based the Geografía universal ilustrada Sopena, this
general geography contains articles on all countries and is
indispensable for school assignments and adult reference.

*Marbán Escobar, Edilberto.   Geografía de América. New
York: Minerva, 1973. 478p.
A basic geography of all the countries of the Americas.
Describes their physical and human geography, and includes
such useful times as national emblems and anthems.

*Marrero y Artiles, Levi.   Viajemos por América. Caracas:
Cultural Venezolana, 1980. 250p. (Colección geografía
visualizada). $D.
This sixth grade-level geography of North America is
useful for assignments and as a refresher source for adults.

*Marrero y Artiles, Levi.   Viajemos por el mundo. Caracas:
Cultural Venezolana, 1980. 248p. (Colección geografía
visualizada). $D.
Similar to Viajemos por América except that the countries are grouped by large geographic area, such as Africa
and Europe.

911—Historical Geography

*Atlas histórico universal Spes. Barcelona: Bibliograf,
1977. 96p. HB. $D.
A historical atlas that includes all countries and
periods, from prehistory to 1975, but emphasizes Spain.
Charts cover chronologies of history, science, technology,
communications, transportation, art, religion, language families, and wars.

912—ATLASES

*Hammond Incorporated.   Atlas moderno universal. Maple-
wood, N.J.: Hammond, 1982. 47p. $E.
A pamphlet-size atlas useful for those not able to
afford the Reader's Digest atlas.

Reader's Digest. **Gran atlas mundial de Selecciones del Reader's Digest.** Madrid: Reader's Digest, 1983. 200p. HB. $B.
Translation of **Reader's Digest Great World Atlas.**

914—TRAVEL IN EUROPE–SPAIN

Carandell, José María. **España, viaje por su vida y su belleza.** Barcelona: Castell, 1980. 124p. HB.
A beautiful photographic work on Spain and its natural and artistic treasures. Includes a short accompanying text. Color photographs. Other titles in this series are: Canada, Japan, China, Mexico.

917.2—TRAVEL IN MEXICO

Asociación Mexicana Automovilistica. **Guía AMA.** México: AMA, 1980. 400p. $D.
A travel guide to Mexico published by the Automobile Club of Mexico. Similar to English language guides available from auto clubs.

918—TRAVEL IN SOUTH AMERICA

Fodor, Eugene. **Guía de Sudamérica.** México: Diana, 1977. 745p.
Fodor's **Guide to South America** in Spanish. There is also a travel guide for Mexico and the United States.

920—BIOGRAPHY

Greene, Jay E. **100 grandes científicos.** México: Diana, 1979. 447p.
A collection of biographies of major scientists, with short individual entries.

Llorca Vilaphana, Carmen. **Las mujeres de los dictadores.**
San Sebastián, Spain: Hyspamérica, 1978. 359p. $C.
Contains biographies of the wives and mistresses of
dictators from antiquity to the present.

*Marbán, Edilberto. **El mundo iberoamericano, hombres en su
historia.** New York: Regents, 1974. 390p. $D.
A collection of excellent biographies of major
personalities from Latin America's past, accompanied by very
good illustrations.

12,000 Minibiografías. México: América, 1984. 800p. $D.
A very handy reference tool containing brief biographies
of historical and contemporary personalities in all fields.

929—GENEALOGY, NAMES, INSIGNIA

Basurto Garća, Carmen. **México y sus símbolos.** México:
Avante, 1979. 279p. $E.
An informative book containing the coats of arms of
Mexican states, biographies of famous Mexicans, and the
flags and national anthem of Mexico. Also provides back-
ground on the origins of various symbols.

929.4—Personal Names

Salazar G., Salvador. **Nombres para el bebé.** New York:
Arco, 1979. 167p. (Guías Fontalba). HB. $D.
Includes Mexican, Italian, and international names.
Also has sections on mythological, Biblical, Saints', and
general names.

929.92—Flags

Inglefield, Eric. **Las banderas.** Barcelona: Fontalba, 1979.
125p. (Guías Fontalba). $D.
Describes international, historical, and U.S. flags.
Also explains symbols and heraldry. Translated from the
British title **Flags.**

940.53—WORLD WAR II

Argyle, Christopher. **Cronología de la II Guerra Mundial, registro ilustrado día por día, 1939-1945.** Bogotá: Educar, 1983. 206p. $C.
A translation of **Chronology of World War II.** A well-illustrated day-by-day account of this drama and its historical settings.

Rothberg, Abraham. **Historia gráfica de la II Guerra Mundial.** Barcelona: Aura, 1980. 4v. $E ea.
A translation of the impressively graphic **Eyewitness History of World War II.**

946—SPANISH HISTORY

Marin, Diego. **La civilización española.** New York: Holt, 1969. 269p. HB. $A.
A standard textbook survey of the major aspects of Spanish civilization. Very useful as an introduction to the subject for students as well as for the general reader.

Molina, M. Isabel. **Historia de un pueblo.** Madrid: Doncel, 1981. 202p. $D.
A well-illustrated and comprehensive short history of Spain, with a special young adult appeal.

970.1—NORTH AMERICAN NATIVE RACES

Gifford, Douglas. **Guerreros, dioses y espíritus de la mitología de América Central y Sudamérica.** Madrid: Anaya, 1984. 132p. $B.
A beautifully illustrated book containing myths and legends of some of the most ancient peoples of Central and South America, such as the Toltecs, Aztecs, Incas, Mayas, and tribes of the Amazon and Argentine pampas. Translation of **Warriors, Gods, and Spirits from Central and South American Mythology.**

972—MEXICO—HISTORY

Fiestas de México. México: Panorama, 1982. 271p. (Guías
   Panorama). $D.
   Translation of **Fiestas in Mexico.** Arranged alphabet-
ically by state. One section describes the major dances of
Mexico. Useful for travelers and as a source of Mexican
folklore. Indexed by state and date of celebration.

Parkes, Henry Banford. **La historia de México.** México:
   Diana, 1979. 475p. $D.
   Translation of the very popular **A History of Mexico,**
first published in 1938.

Paz, Octavio. **El laberinto de la soledad.** México: Fondo de
   Cultura Económica, 1977. 191p. (Colección Popular).
   $E.
   Provides a classic philosophical discussion of Mexican
identity, written by a major Mexican author.

972.003—Mexico—Dictionaries, Encyclopedias, Concordances

**Diccionario Porrúa de historia, biografía y geografía de
   México.** México: Porrúa, 1976. 2v. HB. $A.
   Indispensable for answering biographical, historical,
and geographical questions about Mexico. Includes fold-out
state maps.

972.01—Mexico—Prehistory before European Discovery
       and Conquest

*Chilam Balam Books. **El libro de los libros de Chilam
   Balam.** México: Fondo de Cultura Económica, 1972. 212p.
   $E.
   One of the greatest works of Mayan literature.

Crosher, Judith. **Aztecas.** Barcelona: Molino, 1982. 64p.
   (Pueblos del pasado). HB. $D.
   A pictorial look at the life and customs of the Aztecs.
Especially recommended for younger readers.

León-Portilla, Miguel. **La familia Nahuatl prehispánica.**
   Illustrated by Raúl Guerra Meléndez. México: Instituto
   Nacional Protección Infancia, 1975. 134p.
   Excellent description of pre-Columbian Nahuatl family

life, with attractive color illustrations. Unfortunately, the poor quality paper and magazine format detract from the book's value.

Morley, Sylvanus. **La civilización Maya.** México: Fondo de Cultura Económica, 1980. 527p. HB. $C.
Translation of **The Ancient Maya,** with revisions representing the latest archaeological findings. A serious but readable work on the history and culture of the Mayan people.

*Popol Vuh. México: Porrúa, 1978. 166p. $D.
This famous pre-Columbian literary work contains the creation myth and describes the early historical traditions of the Quiche Mayas of Guatemala. Includes illustrations from early Maya codices. Also published by Fondo de Cultura Económica.

Sodi M., Demetrio. **Las grandes culturas de Mesoamérica: desde la llegada del hombre al continente Americano hasta la última de las culturas prehispánicas.** México: Panorama, 1980. 199p. (Colección Panorama). $D.
Provides a brief but popular description of the major cultures of pre-Columbian America.

Soustelle, Jacques. **La vida cotidiana de los Aztecas.** México: Fondo de Cultura Económica, 1956. 283p. HB. $C.
Based on original documents, this is one of the best secondary sources on the social life and customs of the Aztecs.

Von Hagen, Victor Wolfgang. **El mundo de los Mayas.** México: Diana, 1978. 270p.
Translation of **World of the Mayas.** A readable account of the Mayan civilization.

972.02—Mexico—Conquest and Colonial Period

*Díaz del Castillo, Bernal. **Verdadera historia de los sucesos de la conquista de la nueva España.** Adaptación por Luis Hernández Alfonso. Illustrated by Eduardo Santonja. Madrid: Aguilar, 1965. 110p.
Outstanding adaptation of the classic work written in 1568 by a gentleman who accompanied Cortéz on his New World expeditions from 1519 to 1527. Describes the conquest of Mexico.

972.08—Mexico–Republic, 1867–

Garfias M., Luis. **La revolución Mexicana: compendio histórico político militar.** México: Panorama, 1980. 223p. (Colección Panorama). $D.
A brief, but lively account of the Mexican Revolution.

Guzmán, Martín Luis. **El águila y la serpiente.** México: General, 1971. 455p.
A popular fictionalized account of events of the Mexican Revolution. Considered a classic.

López R., Amalia. **Historia de México de la época prehispánica hasta Juárez.** México: Continental, 1977. 313p. $D.
A basic student–oriented survey of the history of Mexico from its pre–Columbian origins to the presidency of Benito Juárez.

López R., Amalia. **Historia del México contemporáneo.** México: Continental, 1978. 222p. $D.
A short, well–illustrated general history of Mexico from independence to the present. Includes good summaries and basic information on economic and cultural history.

972.85—PUERTO RICAN AND CUBAN HISTORY

Alegría, Ricardo. **Descubrimiento, conquista y colonización de Puerto Rico.** Madrid: Estudios Puertorriqueños, 1971. 175p.
Excellent introduction to the discovery, conquest, and colonization of Puerto Rico, written in a simple, easy-to-understand style for young adults.

Márquez Sterling, Carlos, and Manuel Márquez Sterling. **Historia de la isla de Cuba.** New York: Regents, 1975. 392p. HB. $C.
A well–illustrated, basic, student oriented history of Cuba from its origins to the aftermath of the 1959 revolution.

Neggers, Gladys Crescioni. **Breve introducción a la cultura puertorriqueña.** Madrid: Playor, 1978. 220p. HB. $E.
Attractively presented survey of all important aspects of Puerto Rican culture. Includes a good chronological summary and a basic bibliography.

Thomas, Hugh. **Historia contemporánea de Cuba.** Barcelona:
    Grijalbo, 1982. 567p. $D.
    Translation of **Cuba: the Pursuit of Freedom.** Covers
Cuban history from 1952 to 1982. The author is a British
historian whose research is amply demonstrated in this
objective picture of Cuba.

Vivas Maldonado, José Luis. **Historia de Puerto Rico.** New
    York: Las Américas, 1978. 437p. $B.
    A basic history of Puerto Rico from the earliest times
to the present. Special features are the wealth of additional information—chronologies, summaries, statistics—
included in the appendixes, plus good indexing and bibliographies.

973—UNITED STATES HISTORY

Díaz Cubero José. **Historia del pueblo de los Estados Unidos
    de América.** Madrid: Cultural de Textos Americanos,
    1981. 298p. HB. $C.
    An easy-to-read textbook. Excellent preparation for
citizenship. Chronologically arranged, but has no index.

Historia de los Estados Unidos: la experiencia democrática.
    México: Limusa, 1981. 687p. $A.
    Translation of **The Democratic Experience,** a junior
college textbook.

Wright, Louis B. **Breve historia de los Estados Unidos
    de América.** México: Limusa, 1977. 606p.
    A good, basic history of the United States.

980—GENERAL HISTORY OF SOUTH AMERICA

Descola, Jean. **Los conquistadores del imperio español.**
    Barcelona: Juventud, 1972. 408p. HB. $C.
    The story of the development of Spain's huge empire in
the Americas, told through a series of tales about the major
leaders of the Conquest, such as Cortéz, Pizarro, and
Alvarado. A book with great appeal to young readers.
Translated from the original French.

Descola, Jean. **Los libertadores.** Barcelona: Juventud, 1978. 397p. $C.
A description of the wars for the independence of Spanish America from Spain, centered on the major figures heading the struggle. A work with a special young adult appeal. Translated from the original French.

Montenegro González, Augusto. **Historia de América.** Bogotá: Norma, 1980. 266p. (Nuestro mundo y sus hechos). $D.
A survey history of the Americas, especially useful for its many charts and summaries of events in the history of Spanish America.

Picón Salas, Mariano. **De la conquista a la independencia.** México: Fondo de Cultura Económica, 1978. 261p. $E.
A scholarly but readable landmark work on the history and social life of Latin America during the colonial period.

Rama, Carlos M. **Historia de América Latina.** Barcelona: Bruguera, 1982. 301p. (Libro blanco). $E.
An interdisciplinary history of Latin America from independence to the end of World War II. Follows the common threads and movements of the region.

Rodríguez Lapuente, Manuel. **Historia de Iberoamérica.** Barcelona: Sopena, 1978. 679p. (Biblioteca Hispania Ilustrada). HB. $C.
A profusely illustrated general history of Spanish America that also includes the history of Brazil and other non-Spanish speaking areas.

985.01—PERU-PREHISTORY BEFORE EUROPEAN DISCOVERY AND CONQUEST

Burland, Cottie Arthur. **Incas.** Barcelona: Molino, 1982. 64p. (Pueblos del pasado). HB. $D.
A pictorial look at the daily life of the Incas. Especially recommended for younger readers.

*Von Hagen, Victor Wolfgang. **Los incas: pueblo del sol.** México: Mortiz, 1974. 127p. (Culturas básicas del mundo). $E.
Translation of **Incas, People of the Sun.** A very readable description of the daily life of the Incas, written by a noted journalist. Contains a short, but excellent bibliography of recommended books available in Spanish.

Biography

*Abreu Gómez, Ermilo. **Juárez**. México: Cultura Popular, 1972. 102p.
Excellent biography of Benito Pablo Juárez. ·Describes in simple language his early years in Oaxaca, his education, his political beliefs, and his outstanding contributions to Mexico.

Alavedra, José. **La extraordinaria vida de Pablo Casals**. Barcelona: Ayma, 1969. 121p. $E.
The artistic development of this great Spanish cellist is exquisitely portrayed by the author, who knew Casals.

*Alvarez Coral, Juan. **Compositores mexicanos**. México: Mexicanos Unidos, 1971. 195p. $E.
Contains biographies of Mexican composers.

Anderson Imbert, Enrique. **Genio y figura de Sarmiento**. Buenos Aires: EUDEBA, 1967. 191p. $D.
A well-illustrated presentation of the life and literary work of the great Argentinian statesman Domingo Faustino Sarmiento.

Arcocha, Juan. **Fidel Castro en rompecabezas**. Madrid: Ediciones R., 1973. 126p.
A well-illustrated biography of Fidel Castro.

Cottler, Joseph. **34 biografías de científicos y exploradores**. México: Libro-Mex, 1981. 388p. $E.

Contains biographies of famous explorers, scientists, inventors, biologists, and doctors.

Doig, Desmond. **Madre Teresa de Calcuta: su gente y su obra.** Santander, Spain: Sal Terrae, 1976. 142p. $E.
Describes the work of Mother Teresa among the poor. Many of her experiences as well as her philosophy are told in her own words.

Estenger, Rafael. **La vida gloriosa y triste de Juan Pablo Duarte.** Santo Domingo, Universidad Nacional Pedro Henriquez Ureña, 1981. 205p.
A short, well-presented biography of the father of Dominican independence. A book with special young adult appeal.

Fischer, Louis. **Gandhi.** Buenos Aires, Javier Vergara, 1983. 311p. $D.
Translation of **Gandhi, His Life and Message to the World.** An inspirational account of his life and philosophy.

Fraser, Nicholas. **Eva Perón.** Barcelona: Bruguera, 1982. (Bruguera 5 estrellas). $D
Translation of **Eva Peron.** Details the life of the controversial wife of Argentinian president Juan D. Perón.

*Gallego, Gregorio. **John F. Kennedy.** Madrid: Hernando, 1977. 170p. (Caminos abiertos). $D.
Shows how Kennedy was influenced by his family and other experiences, and describes his impact on the world. Includes articles that provide background on subjects such as political violence, U.S. colonialism in Latin America, civil rights, and the American political process.

*García Rivas, Heriberto. **150 biografías de mexicanos ilustres.** México: Diana, 1973. 262p. $E.
Contains biographies of 150 Mexicans influential in their country's history.

*Garfias, M. Luis. **Verdad y leyendas de Pancho Villa: vida y hechos del famoso personaje de la Revolución Mexicana.** México: Panorama, 1981. 165p. (Colección Panorama). $E.
An objective account that attempts to explode the many myths concerning Villa.

Genios: Goya, Napoleón, Washington, Cervantes, Colón. Barcelona: Sopena, 1975. 708p. (Biblioteca Hispania Ilustrada). $C.

This title, along with **Celebridades** and **Figuras**, provides readable and fairly lengthy articles on the most requested historical figures.

*Howard, Cecil. **Pizarro y la conquista del Perú**. Barcelona: Timun Mas, 1971. 98p. $E.
The conquest of Peru and Pizarro's role as conqueror are portrayed in this fascinating, attractive book. Interesting descriptions and beautiful color photographs are dispersed throughout.

Iglesias, Julio. **Entre el cielo y el infierno**. Barcelona: Planeta, 1981. 287p. $D.
An autobiography by the famous singer.

Lorenzo Sanz, Ricardo. **Simón Bolívar**. Madrid: Hernando, 1978. 161p. (Caminos abiertos). $E.
A biography of the father of Spanish American independence. Includes period background, chronologies, and illustrations.

Marbán Escobar, Edilberto. **El mundo iberoamericano, hombres en su historia**. New York: Regents, 1974. 390p. $C.
This reader contains short biographies of famous Latin Americans.

Márquez Sterling, Carlos. **Martí ciudadano de América**. New York: Las Américas, 1965. 419p. $E.
A good biography of the great Cuban patriot and writer, José Martí. (A more recent edition of this title will be available from Edil in Río Piedras, Puerto Rico.)

Martín Bustamante, Cristina. **Martin Luther King**. Madrid: Hernando, 1977. 168p. (Caminos abiertos). $D.
Places King's life in perspective by analyzing the civil rights situation in the U.S. and how he influenced that movement. To provide background, there are articles on slavery, black poverty, and Gandhi's philosophy of passive resistance.

Martínez, Jesús Manuel. **Juan Pablo II: al servicio de la humanidad**. Barcelona: Castell, 1980. 128p. $D.
A pictorial biography of Pope John Paul II.

Montero, Isaac. **Abraham Lincoln**. Madrid: Hernando, 1976. 161p. (Caminos abiertos). $E.
This biography includes period background and chronologies, and is accompanied by some excellent illustrations.

Orozco L., Fernando. **Grandes personajes de México.** México:
Panorama, 1980. 239p. (Colección Panorama). $E.
Contains biographies of nine of the most important per-
sons in Mexican history.

*Palau y Fabre, José. **La extraordinaria vida de Picasso.**
Barcelona: Ayma, 1972. 100p. $E.
An outstanding biography that explains Picasso's artistic development through the use of excellent photographs of
his greatest works.

Pedreira, Antonio S. **Hostos ciudadano de América.** Río
Piedras, P.R.: Edil, 1968. 167p. $E.
A well-presented account of the life and literary and
political activities of a great Puerto Rican.

Pierri, Ettore. **Vida, pasión y muerte de Emiliano Zapata.**
México: Mexicanos Unidos, 1979. 274p. $E.
A noted journalist uses interviews and primary and sec-
ondary sources to delve into the legend of Zapata.

*Sánchez de Muniain, Blanca. **Sigmund Freud.** Madrid:
Hernando, 1977. 168p. (Caminos abiertos). $D.
A biography of Freud, emphasizing the influences on his
psychological theories and his importance to the development
of psychology.

Verdejo, Carmiña. **Celebridades: Miguel Angel, Francisco
Javier, Santiago Ramón y Cajal, Juana de Arco, Simón
Bolívar.** Barcelona: Sopena, 1978. 671p. (Biblioteca
Hispania Ilustrada). $C.
This title, along with **Genios** and **Figuras**, provides rea-
dable and fairly lengthy articles about the most requested
historical figures.

Verdejo, Carmiña. **Figuras: Edison, Leonardo da Vinci, María
Antonieta, Carlos V, Marco Polo.** Barcelona: Sopena,
1961. 736p. (Biblioteca Hispania Ilustrada). $D.

Villanueva, Jesús. **Julio Iglesias: mi vida.** Barcelona:
Magazin, 1981. 111p. $E.
A pictorial biography of the famous singer.

Fiction for
Young Adults

*Altamirano, Ignacio M. **La navidad en las montañas**. México: Porrúa, 1972. 125p.

A religious novel that describes the author's memories of his town, his parents, and his brother during the happy Christmas celebrations of his youth in 19th century rural Mexico.

Barceló Culleres, Joan. **Ojos de jineta**. Illustrated by Jordi Bulbena. Barcelona: La Galera, 1979. HB. $D.

A fast-moving story relating the abuses and tortures of the Spanish Inquisition. Describes the influence of the belief in magic, witchcraft, astrology and alchemy on the Inquisition.

Blasco Casanovas, Juan. **El rescate del pequeño rey**. Illustrated by Lucía Navarro. Barcelona: La Galera, 1976. 114p. $E

Relates the rescue in 1214 of Jaime I, "The Conqueror," by the heroic efforts of the chivalrous knights Guillermo de Montcada and Rodrigo del Puy. The book is full of daring, adventure, and excitement.

*Cervantes Saavedra, Miguel de. **Aventuras de Don Quijote de la Mancha**. Adaptación de Joaquín Aguirre Bellver. Illustrated by C. Perellón. Madrid: EDAF, 1972. 108p.

The enchanting dialogue and original humor of Cervantes' **Don Quijote** has been maintained in this superb adaptation. Beautifully illustrated.

*Cervantes Saavedra, Miguel de. **Aventuras de Don Quijote para los niños.** Buenos Aires: Editodos, 1978. 61p.
An excellent adaptation for young readers of Cervantes's masterpiece. Includes Don Quijote's well-known adventures in the order in which they appear in the original version. The modern style and vocabulary used in this simplified account make it a most enjoyable and witty introduction.

Gagini, Carlos. **Cuentos y otras prosas.** San José, Costa Rica: Lehmann, 1969. 84p.
Remarkable collection of 14 short stories and four essays by the well-known Costa Rican writer; originally published in the 1920s.

García Márquez, Gabriel. **Relato de un náufrago.** Barcelona: Tusquets, 1984. 128p. $E.
Journalistic report written in 1955 when García Márquez was a young reporter in his native Colombia. It narrates the experiences of a 20-year-old Colombian seaman, Luis Alejandro Velasco, who survived 10 days on a raft at sea without food or water. The account exposes young adults to the robust writing style of this Nobel Prize-winning author.

Garrido de Rodríguez, Neli, ed. **Cuentos de amor para chicos.** Buenos Aires: Orión, 1978. 174p.
Collection of 15 love stories about princes and princesses, legendary characters, and modern boys and girls. The authors include notables such as Rubén Darío, Washington Irving, Alejandro Casona, O. Henry, Victoria Ocampo, Carlos Rodríguez Pintos, Manuel Mújica Lainez, María Domínguez, Susana López de Gómara, Susana Gesumaría and Liliana Aguilar.

Grez, Vicente. **Marianita.** Santiago: Nascimiento, 1976. 200p.
Absorbing love story, originally published in 1885 by the well-known Chilean author. Depicts Chilean society of the 19th century.

Icaza, Jorge. **Huasipungo para niños.** Illustrated by Ramiro Jácome. Adapted by Juan Otrebor and Jorge Icaza. Quito: Casa de la Cultura Ecuatoriana, 1978. 86p.
Excellent adaptation for young adults of the renowned Ecuadorian novel **Huasipungo.** The work is marred only by the poor illustrations of Ecuador.

*Laguerre, Enrique A., ed. **Antología de cuentos puertorriqueños.** México: Orión, 1975. 175p.

Outstanding collection of 20 short stories written by 15 well-known Puerto Rican authors. Includes a few popular Puerto Rican legends and short stories on love, marriage, and mystery.

El lazarillo de Tormes. Adapted by Basilio Losada. Illustrated by C. Sanroma. Barcelona: Aftra, 1975. 166p.
This famous picaresque Spanish novel of the 16th century has been magnificently adapted for adolescents. Describes the adventures of an orphan boy who, alone, must learn to survive in a cruel and difficult world. Delightfully illustrated.

Ledesma, Roberto. **Juan sin miedo.** Buenos Aires: Plus Ultra, 1975. 207p.
Set in Argentina, this adventure story enthralls the reader with its candid characters, its fast-moving action, and its varied scenery.

Méndez Ballester, Manuel. **Isla Cerrera.** Madrid: Pareja, 1941. 285p.
An outstanding historical novel that describes in fascinating detail the early years of Spanish colonial life in Puerto Rico.

Molina, María Isabel. **Balada de un castellano.** Madrid: Doncel, 1970. 92p. $E.
A historical novel of Spain that describes Spanish intrigues, and the life, and customs of the Moors and Christians in the year 990. Includes eight gorgeous illustrations of the library in Cordoba and of the people and cities of Spain.

Quiroga, Horacio. **Los cuentos de mis hijos.** Illustrated by Yenia Dumnova. Montevideo: Arca, 1970. 80p.
Contains ten entertaining animal stories written by the well-known Uruguayan author for his children.

Sierra Fabra, Jordi. **El cazador.** Madrid: S.M., 1981. 213p. $E.
Dubal, a 57-year-old trapper, has never killed an animal in his life. He starts feeling old and decides to go into the forest for the last time to trap a live tiger without any weapons. During the trip, he remembers brief episodes of his life, wondering what he is truly after.

Vallverdú, Josep. **El alcalde chatarra.** Illustrated by Josep Gual. Barcelona: La Galera, 1983. 144p. $E.
Chatarra, a lonely and courageous man, decides to stay

in his town despite the proximity of the enemy's army. He proclaims himself mayor, resolving to save his town from plunder and destruction. There is much action in this warm-hearted story of a man who overcomes his own loneliness and, in doing so, finds happiness.

Vallverdú, Josep. **Cita en la cala negra.** Illustrated by Arcadio Lobato. Barcelona: Noguer, 1982. 133p. $E.

Tomás and Patrick, two teenage boys, are spending their holidays in a resort close to Barcelona. Unexpectedly, they get involved in an exciting mystery--they save Llonch, a wounded man, and later assist the Spanish police in locating a group of thieves and some stolen jewels.

Vallverdú, Josep. **Mir el "ardilla".** Illustrated by Joan Andreu Vallve. Barcelona: La Galera, 1982. 120p. $E.

Life in 11th century Spain is excellently portrayed in this fast-paced story about Moors and Christians. Mir, a brave young boy, and Llop, his father, are repeatedly involved in saving the lives of many Christians as they settle lands that used to belong to the Arabs.

Periodicals

Below is a selected list of the most popular magazines in Spanish. For a more comprehensive list, the reader is referred to the following source: Bibliotecas Para la Gente, comp. **Revistas, an Annotated Bibliography of Spanish-Language Periodicals for Public Libraries.** Berkeley: Univ. of California Pr., 1983. 31p. (Chicano Studies Library Publications series, 9). $E.

BUENHOGAR.

Biweekly. **Good Housekeeping** in Spanish. Second only to **Cosmopolitan en Español** in popularity. Includes fashions, recipes, and serialized novels.

CITA.

Weekly. Photonovel of soap opera romance. Contains one complete story per issue. Extremely popular.

CLAUDIA DE MEXICO.

Monthly. Women's magazine with an emphasis on fashion. Contains articles on different cultures, art, music, travel and other subjects of general interest. Some issues devoted to a particular country or region. Appeals especially to well-educated readers.

COQUETA.

Biweekly. Of special interest to young adult women. Contains a regular article spotlighting a career, as well as articles on grooming, Latin American and U.S.

celebrities; problems of interest to youth, such as dealing with the opposite sex and learning about oneself; and unwed motherhood. One of the magazines in Spanish that appeals specifically to teenagers, but that also has a wider audience of women from age 14 to 35. Very popular.

COSMOPOLITAN EN ESPAÑOL.
Monthly. **Cosmopolitan** in Spanish. A good buy, and extremely popular.

FIESTA.
Weekly. Photonovel of soap opera romance. Contains one long, complete story. Similar to **Linda**. Extremely popular.

INTIMIDADES.
Biweekly. For readers age 15 to late twenties. Small four-by-eight inch format. Contains gossip about celebrities, romantic fiction, feature articles on love and grooming, and a section of sample love letters from readers. Popular.

LINDA.
Weekly. Photonovel of soap opera romance. Contains one long story. Similar to **Fiesta**. Extremely popular.

MECANICA POPULAR.
Monthly. **Popular Mechanics** in Spanish. Moderately popular, but one of the very few clean "men's" magazines.

NOVELA MUSICAL.
Weekly. Photonovel. Contains one complete story based on a popular song.

READER'S DIGEST.
Monthly. Spanish edition.

REVISTA DE GEOGRAFIA UNIVERSAL.
Monthly. Similar to **National Geographic**. Moderately popular.

VANIDADES.
Semimonthly. Extremely popular women's magazine. Has articles on fashion, recipes, gossip, beauty, self-improvement, successful women, politics and culture, and a short novel. Also has the best horoscope in a magazine.

Appendix:
U.S. Distributors
of Spanish Materials

The following is a partial list of distributors of Spanish-language materials in the United States. It is based
primarily on a list published in the **Bulletin** of Proyecto
Leer, and no attempt has been made to investigate the
existence of similar sources all over the country. Often
communities have access to local distributors who do not
advertise nationally, and it would be very difficult, if not
impossible, to establish their existence. Distributors who
specialize mostly in children's books and/or media were not
included because this list is almost entirely dedicated to
adult print materials.

As in any other business, prices, stock size, and trade
practices vary widely among distributors. It is therefore
recommended that buyers request information from two or more
sources before ordering.

Bilingual Publications Co.
1966 Broadway
New York, N Y 10023
    Books published in
    Spain, Latin America,
    and the U.S.

Ediciones Universal
P.O. Box 45353 (Shenandoah)
Miami, FL 33145
    Books about Cuba and
    Cubans; also from Spain
    and Latin America.

Campana Books
601 S. Fifth Avenue
Tucson, AZ 85701
  Mostly books about
  Mexican-Americans; some
  materials published in
  Mexico.

Editorial Excelsior Corp.
2 N. First Street
San Jose, CA 95113
  Books in English and
  Spanish published in
  the U.S. and abroad.

Eliseo Torres
440 Lafayette
New York, NY 10003
  Materials from several
  Spanish-speaking
  countries.

European Book Co.
925 Larkin Street
San Francisco, CA 94109
  Foreign-language
  materials

Hispanic Book Distributors
240 E. Yvon Dr.
Tuczon, AZ 85704
  Materials from Mexico,
  Spain, and the U.S.

Imported Books
P.O. Box 4414
Dallas, TX 75208
  Foreign language books,
  including Spanish.

Lectorum Publications
137 West 14th Street
York, NY 10011
  Books published in
  Latin America and
  Spain.

Libros Españoles
1898 S.W. 8th Street
Miami, FL 33135
  Suppliers of materials
  in print published in
  Spain.

Pan American Book Co.
4362 Melrose Avenue
Los Angeles, CA 90029
  Mostly imported books;
  some published in the
  United States.

Quality Books, Inc.
400 Anthony Trail
Northbrook, IL 60062
  Latin American and
  Spanish materials.

Spanish Book Corp.
  of America
115 Fifth Avenue
New York, NY 10003
  Imported materials
  from Latin America and
  Spain.

Author–Title–Subject Index

Prepared by Schroeder
Editorial Services